Why Christians Should Not Tithe

Why Christians Should Not Tithe
*A History of Tithing and
A Biblical Paradigm for Christian Giving*

JAMES D. QUIGGLE

WIPF & STOCK · Eugene, Oregon

WHY CHRISTIANS SHOULD NOT TITHE
A History of Tithing and A Biblical Paradigm for Christian Giving

Copyright © 2009 James D. Quiggle. All rights reserved. Except for brief quotations in critical publications or reviews, no part of this book may be reproduced in any manner without prior written permission from the publisher. Write: Permissions, Wipf and Stock Publishers, 199 W. 8th Ave., Suite 3, Eugene, OR 97401.

Wipf and Stock Publishers
199 W. 8th Av.e, Suite 3
Eugene, OR 97401

www.wipfandstock.com

ISBN 13: 978-1-60608-926-2

All Scripture quotations, unless otherwise indicated, are taken from the New King James Version®. Copyright © 1982 by Thomas Nelson Inc. Used by permission. All rights reserved.

Other versions that may be quoted are:
The Holy Bible: New International Version (NIV), Copyright 1973, 1978, 1984 by International Bible Society. Used by permission of Zondervan Publishing House. All rights reserved.

Holman Christian Standard Bible (HCSB), Copyright 1999, 2000, 2002, 2003, by Holman Bible Publishers. Scripture quotations marked HCSB are been taken from the Holman Christian Standard Bible®, Copyright © 1999, 2000, 2002, 2003 by Holman Bible Publishers. Used by permission. Holman Christian Standard Bible®, Holman CSB®, and HCSB® are federally registered trademarks of Holman Bible Publishers.

New American Standard Bible Translation, © The Lockman Foundation, 1960, 1962, 1963, 1968, 1971, 1972, 1973, 1975, 1977, 1995. Used by permission. All rights reserved.

Manufactured in the U.S.A.

Contents

Introduction / vii

1. A Necessary Vocabulary Lesson / 1
2. The Tithe in Pre-Mosaic Times / 2
3. The Tithe in Mosaic Times / 9
4. The Tithe in Apostolic Times / 61
5. The Tithe in Post-Apostolic Times / 92
6. A Biblical Paradigm for New Testament Giving / 121

Appendices

    1: Twenty-five reasons New Testament giving is not a tithe / 149

    2: Twenty-five reasons to give the New Testament way / 152

    3: Twenty-one principles of New Testament giving / 155

    4: Christian Giving Calculator, Savings Calculator, Income Calculator / 157

Bibliography / 161

Introduction

Every work has its genesis. In the early years of my Christianity I was troubled by the seeming alchemy whereby apostolic doctrines concerning giving were changed to create a New Testament doctrine of tithing. Precious verses in First and Second Corinthians that taught brotherhood and community were wrested from their context to teach tithing. Old Testament verses commanding a tithe were lain side-by-side with apostolic doctrine in an attempt to create a parallel between the Old Testament tithe and New Testament giving. Dire warnings from Malachi were pronounced against church members who did not give at least ten percent of their income—preferably their gross income. A theologically perverse man-made doctrine taught that the ten percent required by the Law was just a starting point for New Testament believers under grace: as being under grace the believer owes more. That is not grace, it is law deceitfully disguised as grace. These abuses of Scripture and Christians continue today.

The premise of the book is simple: God, having freed his people from the Law through faith in Jesus Christ, does not place on them a burden from the Law (cf. Galatians 5:1). The thesis is equally as simple: Christian giving is not a tithe. Christ challenges the believer to give himself and his possessions to the gospel cause, but the tithe fixes a limit and implies nothing more is needed.

The plan of the book is in several parts: to examine the tithe in Old Testament times; to interpret New Testament scriptures concerning giving; to briefly scan the history of tithing from post-apostolic times to the present; to present a paradigm for Christian giving.

This study views tithing from God's perspective as given in the Scripture. The Jews ignored or modified God's law as suited their worldly needs. In this New Testament age God's principles for Christian giving have been ignored in favor of a legalistic system of giving. These man-made changes to Scripture are generally ignored in this book.

Why Christians Should Not Tithe

May the Holy Spirit illuminate all who come here seeking the truth, and free all those who have been subject to the bondage of men.

1

A Necessary Vocabulary Lesson

THE HEBREW LANGUAGE USED two words to refer to the tithe. The first word was *ma'aser*, a noun meaning "tithe," or "tenth part."[1] The Hebrew word *ma'aser* occurs only in Genesis 14:20; Leviticus 27:30, 31, 32; Numbers 18:21, 24, 26, 28; Deuteronomy 12:6, 11, 17; 14:23, 28; 26:12; 2 Chronicles 31:5, 6, 12; Nehemiah 10:37, 38; 12:44; 13:5, 12; Ezekiel 45:11, 14; Amos 4:4; Malachi 3:8, 10. The other word was *'aser*, a verb meaning "to tithe," "give or take a tithe," or "take a tithe."[2] The Hebrew word *'aser* occurs only in Genesis 28:22; Deuteronomy 14:22; 26:12; 1 Samuel 8:15, 17; Nehemiah 10:37, 38.

The distinction between the noun *ma'aser* and the verb *'aser* is not always observed in the various English translations. Additionally, the use of these words in pre-Mosaic times, Genesis 14:20, 28:22, is not the same as in Mosaic times. In the several discussions to follow in chapters two and three I will explain *ma'aser* and *'aser* in their particular biblical context and historical-cultural milieu.

The New Testament used three Greek words to refer to a tithe. The Greek word *apodekatoo*, "to tithe from," occurs only at Matthew 23:23; Luke 11:42; Luke 18:12; Hebrews 7:5.[3] The word *dekate*, "a tenth part," occurs only at Hebrews 7:2, 4, 8, 9.[4] The word *dekatoo*, "to give or take a tenth," occurs only at Hebrews 7:6, 9.[5] The word *dekatos*, which is the root form of *dekate*, means "tenth" but is never used to refer to a tithe.[6]

---

1. Harris et al., *Wordbook*, 2:704.
2. Ibid.
3. Zodhiates, *Dictionary*, 221.
4. Ibid, 403.
5. Ibid, 404.
6. Ibid. This word occurs only at John 1:39; Revelation 11:13; 21:20.

2

The Tithe in Pre-Mosaic Times

THE TITHE BEFORE ABRAHAM

To tithe is to give a portion of the whole, nominally ten percent, for a religious purpose. The Bible has nothing to say about the tithe during the thousands of years between Adam and Abraham. The documented secular history of giving money and property to support a religious purpose began sometime after the Noahic Flood. "In the ancient Near East lie the origins of a sacral offering or payment of a tenth part of stated goods or property to the deity."[1] In ancient times, in pagan societies, there were national gods, tribal gods, and personal gods. National gods, that is, the people and facilities that managed the worship of these gods, were supported by a portion of civil taxes diverted to religious establishments. In more modern terms, government sponsored worship was supported by government required taxation. This did not preclude voluntary giving, but in practice civil taxation was the primary means of support. That portion of civil taxation which supported religion was called a tithe. Taxation for religious purposes included currency, property (land, buildings, people), the product of industry and trade, and agricultural product consisting of herds, flocks, fruit, nuts, and grains.[2]

The word "tithe" means ten percent. However, the percentage actually given in pre-Mosaic times varied. The amount was always known as a "tithe" but the word became a generalized term meaning giving for a religious purpose. "Often given to the king or to the royal temple, the 'tenth' was usually approximate, not exact. The practice is known from

---

1. Eliade, *Encyclopedia*, 14:537.

2. The term herd(s) indicates domestic cattle and oxen. The term flock(s) indicates domestic sheep and goats.

The Tithe in Pre-Mosaic Times

Mesopotamia, Syria, Palestine, Greece, and as far west as the Phoenician city of Carthage."[3] "While taxation took the form of a tenth, the amount might vary, less or more, though the name ... was retained ... Why a tithe or tenth should have been fixed on so generally is not clear, but it is probably connected with generally primitive views about numbers, or with methods of counting, for example, by fingers and toes."[4]

The tithe came out of such diverse sources as agriculture, fishing, hunting, mining, the spoils of war, and the produce or profits from trading and industry.[5] In ancient Babylon,[6] "kings ... assigned the temples an annual income from the state. When the army won a battle, the first share of the captives and spoils went to the temples ... Certain lands were required to pay to the temples a yearly tribute of dates, corn, or fruit; if they failed, the temples could foreclose on them; and in this way the lands came into possession by the priests."[7] The tithe was offered from the spoils of victory in war,[8] as votive offerings to the gods,[9] and to build temples and statues to the gods.[10] In Sumeria (circa 2500 BC) a tenth of the prisoners captured in battle were offered as sacrifices to the gods.[11] In China the Hsai dynasties (2200–1760 BC) introduced a system of tithes from the produce of the fields.[12]

The *Cyclopedia of Biblical, Theological, and Ecclesiastical Literature*, article "tithe," states, "We must remark that the practice of paying tithes obtained among different nations from the remotest antiquity. Thus the ancient Phoenicians and the Carthaginians sent tithes annually to the Tyrian Hercules (Diod. Sic. 20:14; Justin, 18:7); the southern Arabians could not dispose of their incense before paying a tenth thereof to the

---

3. Eliade, *Encyclopedia*, 14:537.
4. Hastings, *Encyclopedia*, 12:347.
5. Ibid, 12:351.
6. The tithe in Babylon was well established by the time of Hammurabi, who reigned 1848–1806 BC. To put this into biblical perspective, Abram (Abraham) was born in Ur about 1945 BC and arrived in Canaan about 1870 BC (Hollingsworth, *Biblical Chronology*).
7. Durant, *Oriental Heritage*, 233.
8. Hastings, *Encyclopedia*, 12:350, 351.
9. Cary et al., *Dictionary*, 913.
10. Hastings, *Encyclopedia*, 12: 350, 351.
11. Durant, *Oriental Heritage*, 126.
12. Grun, *Timetables*, 3.

priests at Sabota in honor of their god Sabis (Pliny, Hist. iat. 12:32); the ancient Pelasgians paid a tithe of the produce of the soil and the increase of their herds to their deities (Dionys. Halic. 1, 19, 23, etc.); and the Hellenes consecrated to their deities a tenth of their annual produce of the soil (Xenoph. Hellen. 1, 7, 10), of their business profits (Herod. 4:152), of confiscated estates (Xenoph. *Hellen.* 1, 7, 10), of their spoils (Herod. 5, 77; 9:81; Xenoph. *A nab.* 5, 3, 4; *Hellen.* 1.5 3, 21; Diod. Sic. 11:33; Pausan. 3, 18, 5; 5, 10, 4; 10:10, 1; Harpocration, s.v.; and Nobel, *Comment. on Leviticus 27:30*). Among other passages the following may be cited: 1 Macc. 11, 35; Herod. 1, 89; 7:132; Diod. Sic. 5, 421 Pausan. 5, 10, 2; Justin, 20:3; Arist. (*Econ.* 2, 2); Livy, 5, 21; Polyb. 9:39; Cicero, *Veirr.* 2, 3, 6, and 7 (here tithes of wine, oil, and 'minutse bruges' are mentioned); *Pro Leg. Manil.* 6; *Plnt. Ages.* ch. 19:p. 389; Pliny, *Hist. Nat.* 12:14; Macrob. *Sat.* 3, 6; Rose, *Inscr. Gr.* p. 215; Gibbon, 3, 301, ed. Smith; and a remarkable instance of fruits tithed and offered to a deity, and a feast made, of which the people of the district partook, in Xenoph. *A nab.* 5, 3; 9, answering thus to the Hebrew poor man's tithe feast."[13] Throughout history governments and religions have taken a tithe.[14]

ABRAHAM'S TITHE TO MELCHIZEDEK

The first religious offering in the Bible was between Abram and Melchizedek, Genesis 14:20.

> Genesis 14:20, "[Melchizedek said] 'And blessed be God Most High, Who has delivered your enemies into your hand.' And he [Abram] gave him a tithe [*ma'aser*] of all."

The Hebrew text uses the noun form *ma'aser*, "tithe" or "tenth part." When the noun is used what is in view is not the action of giving but the thing given. Abram gave a religious offering in an amount, and consisting of those things, that all present considered appropriately honoring to the God who gave the victory. In the historical-cultural milieu of Abram and Melchizedek (circa 1860 BC) a religious offering need not be exactly ten percent. A portion of the spoils of war was understood by both men as a culturally appropriate expression to thank God for victory in battle. Abram did not need to count out every piece of currency, every suit of

---

13. McClintock and Strong, *Cyclopedia*, 10:144.
14. See also Durant, *Oriental Heritage*, 126, 128, 156, 157, 160–61, 214, 232, 362–63.

armor, every donkey or camel, every "whatever" he gained in his victory. He simply took an amount out of "all" that everyone present recognized as an appropriate religious gift to honor the God who gave the victory.

Why did Abram give a religious gift to God Most High? Abram identified "God Most High, possessor of heaven and earth" with his God YHWH,[15] v. 22. By his religious gift Abram acknowledged God Most High as his God, his victory as coming from his God, and Melchizedek as a representative of his God. Since God Most High-YHWH was the possessor of heaven and earth, then the spoils of war, which were of the earth, and had been received through the victory given by heaven, wholly belonged to YHWH. To give God all was not culturally appropriate, but to give God a portion of all was the centuries old way of honoring one's God.[16]

Why did Abram give his religious gift through Melchizedek? Abram did not owe a tithe or taxes to Melchizedek, the king and high priest of the city of Salem. Abram lived in Hebron, about 20 miles south of Salem, and was not associated with any city-state-kingdom of his time. He owed neither taxes, nor tithe, nor tribute to any king or priest. Abram did not give Melchizedek a tenth part of the spoils because he needed a priestly mediator to speak to God on his behalf: God spoke directly to Abram. Abram did, however, recognize Melchizedek as a genuine representative of YHWH. The blessing given by Melchizedek led Abram to give God a religious offering through Melchizedek.

How does one give a religious offering to God? Abram's answer to this question—a culturally conditioned answer—was to give his offering through God's representative Melchizedek. In light of modern uses for the tithe, we should note that Abram's offering was not intended to support a person, a priesthood, a religious building, or a religious ministry.[17] Undoubtedly Melchizedek did put this offering to some such use. What Abram intended was to pointedly acknowledge God Most High-YHWH

---

15. YHWH is an ancient Hebrew word for God. In many English versions YHWH appears as Yahweh, Jehovah, or LORD.

16. Wenham, *Genesis 1–15*, 317, "Tithing was an old and widespread custom in the ancient orient. Tithes were given to both sanctuaries and kings. Melchizedek qualifies on both counts."

17. Because some modern denominations reference Abraham's tithe as justification to require a regular tithe to financially support their churches, it is important to notice that Abraham did not tithe from his regular earnings. To put it into modern terms, Abraham gave a tithe from a bonus (the spoils of war).

as his personal God. His *ma'aser* made a clear statement that he owed allegiance to no other god or person.[18]

JACOB'S TITHE

The next occurrence of a religious offering is Genesis 28:20–22.

> Genesis 28:20–22, "If God will be with me, and keep me in this way that I am going, and give me bread to eat and clothing to put on, so that I come back to my father's house in peace, then YHWH shall be my God. And this stone which I have set as a pillar shall be God's house, and of all that You give me I will surely give a tenth ['*aser*] to You."

The Hebrew text uses the verb form, '*aser*, "give a tithe," versus the NKJV, NIV, HCSB, and NASB95 translation "give a tenth." When the verb form is used what is in view is not the thing given, but the action of giving. What was important to Jacob was not the amount, as the translation "tenth" suggests, but act of giving the offering. One must keep in mind that the word "tithe" in Jacob's historical-cultural milieu (circa 1700 BC) did not bear the same meaning it took on under the Mosaic Law (circa 1445 BC). Jacob wasn't thinking of ten percent, he was thinking that giving God a portion of the spoils was an appropriate way to honor God. He would do what Abraham (who died when Jacob was about fifteen) had done: honor God with a portion of those things God had given him. Jacob, on his way to Haran, had a vision of God's protection. Following the vision Jacob made a vow to YHWH in a place called Bethel, and he built an altar and poured oil on the altar to solemnize his vow. Jacob vowed, "I will surely 'give a tithe' ['*aser*] to you." Jacob returned to Bethel about twenty years later, rebuilt the altar (Genesis 35), and offered a sacrifice of thanks (drink and oil offerings). However, fulfillment of the vow is never mentioned. How could Jacob give a tithe to God? No priest is mentioned, and indeed, none was needed, because God spoke directly with Jacob. Jacob owed neither taxes, nor tithes, nor tribute to any king. There was no religious building, other than the simple altar. The only worshipers of YHWH known to be present were himself and his immediate family (Isaac and Esau were alive but not mentioned as present). There was

---

18. Compare Abram's response to the King of Sodom. By denying a portion of the spoils to the King of Sodom, Abram is culturally stating that the King is not his king, and the King's gods are not his gods.

no religious organization or priest to whom Jacob might give a tithe. He seems to have remembered his vow, Genesis 35:1–3, 7, 14–15. How, then, did Jacob keep his vow? Scripture does not say. Nor is it appropriate to suggest that God took his tithe by allowing troubled times to come upon Jacob and his house. Scripture never states a penalty for failure to tithe.[19]

JOSEPH'S TAX

Joseph is not known for giving a tithe, but he is known for establishing a tax. A portion of that tax would have been used to support the religious systems of Egypt. The cultural expectations of the times would indicate Pharaoh was already collecting taxes, which were used to support the government and government-sponsored religion. Joseph's one-fifth (twenty percent) tax would be added to existing taxes, Genesis 47:24. "And it shall come to pass in the harvest that you [Israel] shall give one-fifth to Pharaoh. Four-fifths shall be your own, as seed for the field and for your food, for those of your households and as food for your little ones."

Joseph's tax was on food, not money. His tax was intended to supply food to Egypt during the prophesied seven years of famine, and was therefore collected in advance of the famine. A tax of food seems to have been the practice of ancient Egypt. Maspero[20] speaks of a ten percent tax on the gross product of the land. Taxes were paid in grains, beans, and field produce. Those (husband, wife, children) who could not pay, because of drought or disease (in the crops) were jailed, enslaved, or killed and their lands seized by the state. Maspero's method of presenting history does not indicate a specific time period, but it would seem that this was the practice from very ancient times. Joseph's tax was part of his culture, and the diversion of part of that tax to support the religious establishment would have been the expectation of all.

SUMMARY AND LESSONS LEARNED

Secular history plainly reveals that "tithe" was the term used to identify religious giving. The tithe was usually a part of taxes in general, a portion of which, a tithe, was set aside to support the religious establishment. In some cases the religious establishment, acting under civil authority, collected the religious offering directly. The amount of any one tithe was

---

19. See chapter three, section, "Was Tithing a Legal Requirement?"
20. Maspero, *Dawn*, 330–32.

approximate, not an exact ten percent. Any religious offering required by civil or religious authority was a "tithe."

The first biblical mention of a tithe was Abram's tithe to Melchizedek. The biblical text does not explain Abram's action, which would indicate religious giving was an established cultural practice; an assumption agreeable to what is known about the tithe in secular history. Abram's tithe was an appropriate way to honor the God who had given him victory over his enemies. Since Melchizedek was a representative of Abram's God, then he was an appropriate recipient of Abram's offering. Abram's offering establishes a biblical principle. A religious offering is an appropriate means to recognize that the whole belongs to YHWH, who possesses heaven and earth. Jacob was also culturally influenced, perhaps remembering the story of Abram's tithe to Melchizedek. Jacob used a religious offering as a means to acknowledge YHWH as his God and protector, promising to give a tenth to YHWH out of all YHWH gave him. Joseph's tax was not a tithe, but because religion was supported by the government, Joseph's tax would have been used to support the Egyptian religious system.

These are the lessons learned. All one has in the world comes from God. Giving a portion of the whole to God's representative is an appropriate way to acknowledge God as possessor of heaven and earth and as one's personal God. A religious offering is an appropriate means to return thanks for personal blessings. A modern application may be made from Joseph's tax. Jacob and his family were required to pay Joseph's twenty percent tax, part of which would be used to support a religious system opposed to their faith in YHWH. The believer is responsible to obey the law of the land and pay taxes; governments are responsible to use taxes in ways that honor the one true God.

3

The Tithe in Mosaic Times

THE MODERN CALENDAR AND ISRAEL'S FESTIVALS AND HARVESTS

A COMPLETE UNDERSTANDING OF the Mosaic Tithes requires an understanding of the relationship of modern months to the three mandatory festivals and the crop harvests. The Jewish calendar was based on a lunar cycle of twenty-eight days. The old month ended and a new month began at the first sighting of the sliver of the waxing crescent moon after the new moon.[1] Because of the lunar cycle, Jewish months began and ended about half-way through the months on the modern calendar. The following table shows the relationship between modern months and the Jewish harvests and mandatory festivals.

Modern Month	Mandatory Festival	Harvest
mid-March—mid-April	Passover-Unleavened Bread	Barley
mid-April—mid-May		Wheat/Oats
mid-May—mid-June	Pentecost	Peas/Lentils/Vetch
mid-June—mid-July		Chickpeas/Grapes
mid-July—mid-August		Sesame/Flax/Millet/Grapes
mid-August—mid-September		Grapes/Figs/Pomegranates
mid-September—mid-October	Trumpets, Atonement, Tabernacles	Grapes/Olives
mid-October—mid-November		Olives

---

1. A new moon is when the moon is between the earth and the sun. In this alignment the sun cannot shine on the side of the moon facing the earth.

From mid-November through mid-March there were no harvests and no festivals. The last month of the Jewish year corresponded to the modern mid-February—mid-March.

THE TITHE IN THE LAW OF MOSES

Israel's experience in Egypt had prepared them to expect a god whom they could see (an idol) and whom they could propitiate by sacrifice and good works. In relation to the worship of YHWH they were spiritually inexperienced and immature (Galatians 3:19–25). God gave them a path, the Law, which if faithfully followed would bring them safely (morally and spiritually) to their Messiah (Galatians 3:23–24). A religious offering to YHWH was part of that Law, and indeed the Israelites would have expected their God to require a tithe. A tithe, in their experience, supported government and religion. The tithe YHWH imposed supported their new religion of YHWH worship by supporting the tribe of Levi who led them in that worship. Since Israel's government was a mediated theocracy, the tithe supported the government by supporting the worship of YHWH. To a spiritually immature people God gave a path of life that encompassed their civil and religious responsibilities. Like every other part of the Law, the regulations concerning the tithe prescribed the behavior expected: the things to be tithed and the amount to be given.[2]

The philosophic basis for the Mosaic tithe was the principle established by Abraham's tithe to Melchizedek: YHWH is the possessor of heaven and earth. In the Law, however, this principle is more closely defined. YHWH is the owner of the land he is giving to Israel, Leviticus 23:23. The Israelites are tenants on YHWH's land. Therefore Israel owes YHWH a tithe:

> Leviticus 27:30–33, "And all the tithe [ma'aser] of the land, whether of the seed of the land or of the fruit of the tree, is the Lord's. It is holy to the Lord. If a man wants at all to redeem any of his tithes [ma'aser], he shall add one-fifth to it. And concerning the tithe [ma'aser] of the herd or the flock, of whatever passes under the rod, the tenth ['asiriya] one shall be holy to the Lord. He shall not inquire whether it is good or bad, nor shall he exchange it; and if he exchanges it at all, then both it and the one exchanged for it shall be holy; it shall not be redeemed."

---

2. The tithe, as part of the Law, is subject to the logic of Galatians 3:24–25, a discussion for the fourth chapter.

The Tithe in Mosaic Times

These first basic instructions were later amplified in Numbers and Deuteronomy. In the preceding chapter I examined the individual occurrences of *ma'aser* and *'aser*. In this chapter I will ask a series of questions and incorporate the instructions from Leviticus, Numbers, and Deuteronomy into the answers.

WHAT WAS TITHED?

The tithe was taken out of the agricultural product of the land. The tithe came out of the grains, fruits (including wine, oil[3]), nuts, herds, and flocks, Leviticus 27:30–32; Deuteronomy 12:17; 14:22–23. Since Israel's economy was dominated by agricultural products, it was reasonable a tithe should come out of the products of that economy. The economy also employed gold and silver smiths, weavers, those who made clothes and those who made shoes, metal workers, clay pot makers, those who spun wool and those who dyed wool, bankers, merchants, soldiers, politicians, priests, religious workers, and other makers and sellers of goods and services. The majority of the people, however, were farmers and ranchers.

It is important to grasp that the tithe was from the grains, fruits, nuts, sheep, goats, cattle, and oxen *only*. Although there were employments other than farming and ranching, resulting in other types of income, the tithe concerned only these products of the agricultural economy. The exchange of money was the basis of economic transactions, but money was not tithed. Money in the form of coins was invented in China in 900 BC and in the biblical world about 700 BC.[4] However, pieces of metal (such as silver arm bands designed so that pieces could be broken off as payment) were being used as early as 5000 BC. To put this into the biblical context, Moses lived about 1500 BC. Cultures as early as 3000 BC were using precious metals and letters of credit as forms of payment. Money today has an artificial value set by constantly changing economic factors. In the ancient world, precious metals (and later, coins made of precious metals) were the form of currency. Each precious metal had a certain economic value

---

3. Wine came from grapes and other fruit, oil from olives. Wine and oil were not tithed as the products of a manufacturing process but as part of the harvest. Changing fruit into wine (fermented or non-fermented) and olives into oil were methods of preserving the products of the field for storage and later use.

4. Paper money was invented in China circa AD 600 because of a shortage of precious metals for coins, but was not used in general circulation until circa AD 900. Paper money was introduced into Europe in the late 1600s and in America in the early 1700s.

by weight. To control costs, the governments of the ancient Babylonians, Egyptians, and Sumerians, circa 3000 BC, established a standard unit of weight by which to measure the value of precious metals for use in commerce and taxation. The standard for Israel was the *shekel*, a unit of weight to measure precious metals for use in commerce and taxation.

The tithe of the herds (*baqar*) was from domesticated cattle and oxen. The tithe from the flocks (*so'n*) was from domesticated sheep and goats. The word *'asiriya*, which is the number ten, was used to describe the tithe from the herds and flocks, Leviticus 27:32. The herd or flock was made to pass "under the rod," meaning that the animals passed one by one through some sort of narrow structure. Every tenth, *'asiriya*, animal was marked in some fashion to be given as a tenth part, *ma'aser*, of the whole. If a flock of thirty-nine sheep passed under the rod, then the tithe from that flock was three sheep.

The food crops given in First Tithe could be "redeemed," *ga'al*, Leviticus 27:31, that is, the tither could buy back the food crop tithe from the Lord. To calculate the redemption price a priest would value the tithe in terms of money, and then add to that valuation an additional one-fifth (twenty percent) of the total value. So, if a tithe of grain was valued at five shekels, it could be redeemed for six shekels; if valued at 100 shekels the redemption price was 120 shekels. This redemption money was not a tithe; it was given in lieu of the tithe. A tithe from the herds and flocks could not be redeemed, v. 33. Additionally, if the animal to be tithed was sickly or maimed it could not be changed for a healthier animal. If such a change was attempted both animals were given as part of the tithe. Products that might come from these animals, such as meat, wool, leather, etc., were not tithed.

HOW MANY TITHES WERE GIVEN?

The items to be tithed are very generally described at Leviticus 27:30–33. The tithes are described in more detail in Numbers and Deuteronomy. There were four distinct tithes. To avoid confusion I will name them First Tithe, Levites' Tithe, Festival Tithe, and Poor Tithe. First Tithe was given by Israel to the Levites and is described in Numbers 18:21–24.

> Numbers 18:21–24, "Behold, I have given the children of Levi all the tithes [*ma'aser*] in Israel as an inheritance in return for the work which they perform, the work of the tabernacle of meeting.

The Tithe in Mosaic Times

> Hereafter the children of Israel shall not come near the tabernacle of meeting, lest they bear sin and die. But the Levites shall perform the work of the tabernacle of meeting, and they shall bear their iniquity; it shall be a statute forever, throughout your generations, that among the children of Israel they shall have no inheritance. For the tithes [ma'aser] of the children of Israel, which they offer up as a heave offering to the Lord, I have given to the Levites as an inheritance; therefore I have said to them, 'Among the children of Israel they shall have no inheritance.'"

Levites' Tithe was given to the priests by the Levites and is described in Numbers 18:25–32. The Levites' tithe was one-tenth of the grain, fruits, and nuts of First Tithe.

> Numbers 18:25–30, "Then the Lord spoke to Moses, saying, 'Speak thus to the Levites, and say to them: 'When you take from the children of Israel the tithes [ma'aser] which I have given you from them as your inheritance, then you shall offer up a heave offering of it to the Lord, a tenth [ma'aser] of the tithe [ma'aser]. And your heave offering shall be reckoned to you as though it were the grain of the threshing floor and as the fullness of the winepress. Thus you shall also offer a heave offering to the Lord from all your tithes [ma'aser] which you receive from the children of Israel, and you shall give the Lord's heave offering from it to Aaron the priest. Of all your gifts you shall offer up every heave offering due to the Lord, from all the best of them, the consecrated part of them.' Therefore you shall say to them: 'When you have lifted up the best of it, then the rest shall be accounted to the Levites as the produce of the threshing floor and as the produce of the winepress.'"

Festival Tithe was given three times a year by the tither to himself to be used by him and his family at the three mandatory festivals. Festival Tithe is described in Deuteronomy 12:6–7, 11–12, 17–21; 14:22–26.

> Deuteronomy 12:6–7, "here [Jerusalem] you shall take your burnt offerings, your sacrifices, your tithes [ma'aser], the heave offerings of your hand, your vowed offerings, your freewill offerings, and the firstborn of your herds and flocks. And there you shall eat before the Lord your God, and you shall rejoice in all to which you have put your hand, you and your households, in which the Lord your God has blessed you."

> Deuteronomy 12:11–12, "then there will be the place [Jerusalem] where the Lord your God chooses to make His name abide. There

you shall bring all that I command you: your burnt offerings, your sacrifices, your tithes [ma'aser], the heave offerings of your hand, and all your choice offerings which you vow to the Lord. And you shall rejoice before the Lord your God, you and your sons and your daughters, your male and female servants, and the Levite who is within your gates, since he has no portion nor inheritance with you."

Deuteronomy 12:17–18, "You may not eat within your gates the tithe [ma'aser] of your grain or your new wine or your oil, of the firstborn of your herd or your flock, of any of your offerings which you vow, of your freewill offerings, or of the heave offering of your hand. But you must eat them before the Lord your God in the place which the Lord your God chooses, you and your son and your daughter, your male servant and your female servant, and the Levite who is within your gates; and you shall rejoice before the Lord your God in all to which you put your hands."

Deuteronomy 14:22–26, "You shall truly ['aser] tithe ['aser] all the increase of your grain that the field produces year by year. And you shall eat before the Lord your God, in the place where He chooses to make His name abide, the tithe [ma'aser] of your grain and your new wine and your oil, of the firstborn of your herds and your flocks, that you may learn to fear the Lord your God always. But if the journey is too long for you, so that you are not able to carry the tithe,[5] or if the place where the Lord your God chooses to put His name is too far from you, when the Lord your God has blessed you, then you shall exchange it for money, take the money in your hand, and go to the place which the Lord your God chooses. And you shall spend that money for whatever your heart desires: for oxen or sheep, for wine or similar drink, for whatever your heart desires; you shall eat there before the Lord your God, and you shall rejoice, you and your household."

Poor Tithe was given in years three and six of the Sabbath cycle for the arable land (I will explain the Sabbath cycle later in this chapter). Poor Tithe is described in Deuteronomy 14:27–29; 26:12–14.

Deuteronomy 14:27–29, "You shall not forsake the Levite who is within your gates, for he has no part nor inheritance with you. At the end of every third year you shall bring out the tithe [ma'aser] of your produce of that year and store it up within your gates. And

---

5. The words ma'aser or 'aser are not in the text but the word "carry," nasa, is in a grammatical form that refers back to the word ma'aser in v. 23.

The Tithe in Mosaic Times

the Levite, because he has no portion nor inheritance with you, and the stranger and the fatherless and the widow who are within your gates, may come and eat and be satisfied, that the Lord your God may bless you in all the work of your hand which you do."

Deuteronomy 26:12–14, "When you have finished laying aside ['*aser*] all the tithe [*ma'aser*] of your increase in the third year—the year of tithing [*ma'aser*]—and have given it to the Levite, the stranger, the fatherless, and the widow, so that they may eat within your gates and be filled, then you shall say before the Lord your God: 'I have removed the holy *tithe* [word not present in the original text] from my house, and also have given them to the Levite, the stranger, the fatherless, and the widow, according to all Your commandments which You have commanded me; I have not transgressed Your commandments, nor have I forgotten them. I have not eaten any of it when in mourning, nor have I removed any of it for an unclean use, nor given any of it for the dead. I have obeyed the voice of the Lord my God, and have done according to all that You have commanded me.'"

First Tithe (Numbers 18:21–24) was the tithe the Levites received from the other tribes for themselves. The First Tithe was considered a heave offering from Israel to the Lord, Numbers 18:24.[6] This tithe was ten percent of the grains, fruits, and nuts, and ten percent of the animals raised by the farmer/rancher (hereinafter, farmer). There is some question as to whether or not animals were part of First Tithe. The Mishnah tractates on tithing[7] do not mention animals as part of First Tithe, nor part of Levites' Tithe. The priests ate meat from the altar, and had lands[8] on which to raise animals, so animals were not needed in the Levites' Tithe. The Levites shared the land with the priests, but First Tithe would supplement their meat supplies in the same way the sacrifices on the altar

---

6. The First Tithe was a heave offering for two reasons. First, the tithe from the land and animals belonged to the Lord, the Lord was the inheritance of the tribe of Levi, so the tithe from the land and animals was a heave offering to the Lord. Second, the Levites Tithe, which came out of the First Tithe, was a heave offering to the priests, therefore the whole was holy to the Lord.

7. Mishnah, tractates *Demai, Maaseroth, Maasser*. The Mishna is a Jewish commentary on the Law compiled from Rabbinic oral and written teaching and commentary extending from approximately 200 BC to AD 200.

8. The tribe of Levi did not have assigned territories like the other tribes, but did have land associated with their assigned cities, Numbers 35:3, "for their cattle, for their herds, and for all their animals."

supplemented the priests. In my view the phrase "all the tithes in Israel," Numbers 18:21, references Leviticus 27:30–32 and indicates First Tithe included the herds and flocks.

Did tenant farmers tithe First Tithe? This question cannot be answered directly from Scripture so we must reason from the scriptures. There are two possibilities. One, the agricultural product was apportioned between owner and tenant before the tithe, and the owner tithed on the portion he received and his tenants tithed on the portion they retained for themselves. Two, the agricultural product was tithed before it was apportioned between tenant and owner. The second solution seems the simplest, and therefore the most likely.

Levites' Tithe (Numbers 18:25–30) is as "the grain of the threshing floor and as the fullness of the winepress," indicating this tithe was from food crops only (no animals). Levites' Tithe was what the Levites gave the priests out of First Tithe. The priests were the male members of the family of Aaron in the tribe of Levi. The Levites were all the members of the tribe of Levi except the family of Aaron. Levites' Tithe was a "tithe of the tithe," Numbers 18:26. The Levites took First Tithe from the other tribes. Then they took a tenth out of First Tithe (food crops only) and gave it to the priests as a heave offering to the Lord.[9] A heave offering was a part of an offering that was lifted up to the Lord and belonged to the priests. The Levites were to tithe from the best of the tithe they had received. If from the best, then it would be accounted as though they had given the whole, as though it had come from their own threshing floors and winepresses.

Festival Tithe was given by all tribes except Levi, Deuteronomy 12:6–7, 11–12, 17–21; 14:22–26. This tithe was used to support the worshiper at the three mandatory festivals (Exodus 23:14–17; Deuteronomy 16:16), which is why I have named it Festival Tithe. This tithe was brought by the farmer to each of the three mandatory festivals to provide food and drink for him and his family. This tithe included animals. According to Deuteronomy 12:6–7, 17–18; 14:22, the firstlings of the animals were tithed for Festival Tithe.[10] The Lord made a provision, 14:24, to convert Festival tithe to money for those who would have a long journey to

---

9. Thus, in giving the First Tithe the other tribes retained ninety percent of their crops and herds. In giving the Levites' Tithe the Levites retained ninety percent of what they received from the fields in First Tithe, and one hundred percent of the herds and flocks received in First Tithe.

10. See below, section, "When Were the Animals Tithed?"

The Tithe in Mosaic Times

Jerusalem. This is not the same as the redemption provision for First Tithe in Leviticus 27:31. First Tithe food crops could be redeemed, *ga'al*, for their value plus an added twenty percent and the money given in lieu of the crops. Animals given in First Tithe could not be redeemed. However, all of the Festival Tithe, food crops and animals, could be exchanged, *nathan*, for money. When the farmer arrived at Jerusalem he was to use all that money to buy food (which could include animals, v. 26) and drink, 14:25–26. Because in modern times we are too used to thinking of a tithe as always given to others, it is important to understand that the Festival Tithe was kept by the person making the tithe, to provide him and his family food and drink during their stay at Jerusalem.

Did the tenant farmer make a Festival Tithe? Again, Scripture does not address tenant farmers, but we can reason from the scriptures. Every male was required to come to the mandatory festivals, therefore every farmer, tenant or owner, was required to bring a Festival Tithe. The tenant farmer tithed a Festival Tithe out of his portion. Did non-farmers (city dwellers) tithe a Festival Tithe? Since city dwellers did not produce agricultural product, then they had no product from which to make a Festival Tithe. The reasonable solution is that city dwellers either brought food with them or bought food in Jerusalem during the festivals.

Festival Tithe is described in Deuteronomy 14:22 in these words: "You shall truly [*'aser*] tithe [*'aser*] all the increase of your grain that the field produces year by year." The words "truly tithe" are the translation of two different grammatical forms of the word *'aser*. This verse literally reads, "You shall tithe a tithe all the increase of your grain that the field produces year by year." The word translated "increase" in the NKJV (NIV, HCSB, NASB95: produce) is *t^ebu'a*. The word does not mean an increase over what was sown, or an increase over the previous year, but simply means the total yield of the field, whether grain or fruit.[11] The point of the "truly tithe" instruction was to emphasize that this tithe must be given, even though it was for personal use at the festivals. Some commentators believe Festival Tithe was given once a year, based on a certain view of 14:22. However, since the farmer was to give himself a tithe to take to Jerusalem for his use at each mandatory festival, 14:23, then he must make three separate tithes, one for each festival. Therefore, Festival Tithe was taken three times a year (March-April, May-June, September-October) from the

---

11. Harris et al., *Wordbook*, 1:95.

appropriate harvest (or previously harvested and stored grain, fruit, nuts). Some commentators believe Festival Tithe was used at Jerusalem during the three mandatory festivals and at the farmer's home city for all other festivals. However, the instruction at 14:23 (and the similar instructions in chapter 12) indicates only the mandatory festivals are in view.

The Israelites, except the tribe of Levi, were to make a tithe to support the poor in the land, Deuteronomy 14:27–29; 26:12–14, which is why I have named it Poor Tithe. This tithe did not include animals. This tithe was given at the end of the year in years three and six of the seven year Sabbath cycle for the arable land. Poor Tithe was made in a month when there were no harvests and no festivals. The first harvests of the year were barley in March-April and wheat in May-June. The last harvests of the year were of various fruits and olives from September into November. The end of the year was February-March. Because Poor Tithe was given at the end of the year it did not interfere with First Tithe, which was taken at the end of each harvest, nor Festival Tithe, which was taken out of the appropriate harvest three times during the year. The end-of-the-year Poor Tithe would be small, but diverse, because taken from the stored remains of all the harvests reaped, threshed, and stored throughout the year. By giving Poor Tithe at the end of years three and six it would contribute to the needs of the poor at the midway point of the Sabbath cycle and during the fallow seventh year. A recap will put the Poor Tithe into perspective. Throughout the year the Levites took ten percent out of the various harvests, leaving ninety percent for the farmer. Three times during the year the farmer took ten percent of that ninety percent for his own use during the three mandatory festivals. Then, at the end of years three and six, the farmer took ten percent out of whatever remained in storage from all the previous harvests and gave it as a tithe for the poor. Did the tenant farmer tithe Poor Tithe? Poor Tithe was not made from any particular harvest but from stored food crops. The owner might live on a farm, or might be a city dweller and have little or no storage. The tenant, who lived on the farm, would have stored food crops. Probably both were responsible to make Poor Tithe out of whatever food each had stored from previous harvests.

The Poor Tithe was stored "within your gates." Most cities in the ancient world were surrounded by a wall that had one or more gates for entry. Usually, a common market place was located just inside the main gate. The leaders of the city, in modern terms the mayor and city council,

The Tithe in Mosaic Times

would meet at the gates (near the market place) to publically conduct city business. The public also commonly conducted various personal legal and business affairs at the gates. The book of Ruth, 4:1–12, provides an example during the time of the judges. The city gates came to be used as a symbol for the city. To store the tithe for the poor "within your gates," meant Poor Tithe was to be stored within the city walls—inside the city—for disbursement to the poor (Levite, stranger, fatherless, widow) living in that city.

Some commentators question as to whether Deuteronomy 14:27, "you shall not forsake the Levite who is within your gates," belongs with the instructions for Festival Tithe or Poor Tithe. However, Festival Tithe was to be eaten only at "the place where God chooses to make his name abide," v. 23, which was Jerusalem (1 Kings 11:36). The reference to the Levite in v. 27 is to "the Levite who is within your gates." The identity of "you" and "your" in v. 27 is established in v. 22 as the farmer who is making the tithes, and so on throughout vv. 22–29. The Levite "within your gates" is a reference to a Levite living in the farmer's city, and thus v. 27 is properly associated with the instructions for the Poor Tithe.[12] This Levite, if he were poor, would be eligible to receive the tithe for the poor that the farmer was, v. 28, to store within your (the farmer's) city. Since Poor Tithe was stored in the city, the city elders would control the disbursement. The elders were responsible to ensure Poor Tithe was used to support the poor stranger (non-Israelite), the fatherless, the widow, and any poor Levite living in their city. A Levite living in a city other than one of the cities assigned to the tribe of Levi might be among the poor (despite First Tithe), since he (conceivably) would not have lands from which to supplement his living. The intent of v. 27 is to ensure each Levite received proper support so he could focus on his work in the temple.

The Festival Tithe is described as, "the tithe of your grain and your new wine and your oil, and the firstlings of your flocks and herds," Deuteronomy 14:23. The Poor Tithe is described as, "your produce of that year," Deuteronomy 14:28. The word "produce" is used to describe grain,

---

12. Could Festival Tithe have been intended to also support the Levites during the festivals? More priests would be needed during festivals to accommodate the increased numbers of worshipers and sacrifices, thus it is possible that more Levites would be needed in Jerusalem during festivals than at other times. If some tithes were stored in the temple, then they would be provided their daily sustenance from those stores. If Festival Tithe was shared with the Levites Scripture gives no guidance as to an equitable distribution.

fruit, and nuts, excluding herds and flocks, for example, Numbers 18:30; Deuteronomy 28:51. Therefore, although Festival Tithe included animals, Poor Tithe did not include animals. This is because agricultural product could be stored long-term but meat could not, and there was no provision in the Law requiring city elders to manage a flock or herd to feed the poor. In the ancient world meat was not the daily staple it is today, so this did not create a hardship for the poor.

In the third and sixth years did the farmer give both a Festival Tithe and a Poor Tithe? An argument against giving both Festival and Poor tithes in the same year is that this would place a cumulative tithe burden of twenty-seven percent on the farmer (First+Festival+Poor=27%). However, the argument is without merit. The total burden of the three tithes only seems to add up to a burden of twenty-seven percent. In reality the tithes were not cumulative. The losses from tithing were only ten percent in any given month. First Tithe was given only when the farmer had a harvest and after weaning animals (see discussions below, "How was the Tithe Given?" and "When was the Agricultural Product Tithed?"). In the three months where both First Tithe and Festival Tithe might be given at the same time,[13] the tithe burden was nineteen percent.[14] However, Festival Tithe was not a loss to the farmer as was First Tithe. In Festival Tithe the farmer paid himself, which was food he would have used for himself (to eat or sell) under any circumstances. Therefore, Festival Tithe was no loss to the farmer. When Poor Tithe was paid it was in a month when there were no other tithes, so the loss in that month was ten percent. The tithe burden can't really be measured as a cumulative twenty-seven percent loss. In very practical terms the loss due to tithing was only the ten percent paid to the Levites in First Tithe during the eight months of harvests (assuming a farmer had a harvest in each month), and ten percent for Poor Tithe every third and sixth years in the last month of the year.

---

13. First Tithe would be given in the same month as Festival Tithe only if a farmer had a harvest in one of the three months in which there was a festival. Not every farmer would grow every product. To make a Festival Tithe in a month when he did not have a harvest a farmer could gather the tithe from stored food crops.

14. Some commentators believe First Tithe and Festival Tithe were once a year events. For example, Christensen, *Deuteronomy 1:1–21:9*, 303–305; Keil and Delitszch, *Commentary*, 1:917. This seems unlikely for reasons discussed in sections "How was the Tithe Given?" and "When was the Agricultural Product Tithed?"

The Tithe in Mosaic Times

Good arguments may be made for Festival Tithe being given in the same years Poor Tithe was given. It seems reasonable that the farmer made his Festival Tithe just before the festival for which the tithe was intended. This would mean Festival Tithe was made three times each year, once each out of the harvests associated with the festivals of Unleavened Bread, Pentecost, and Tabernacles. These tithes would be from the barley, wheat, and fruit harvests, respectively, and firstlings from the herd and flock. One must also consider that the three festivals were held every year, and attendance was mandatory (for males), which argues that Festival Tithe continued to be made in those years when Poor Tithe was given. As to the Poor Tithe, without question the farmer stored for his own use all produce he did not sell or did not tithe in First Tithe and Festival Tithe. This means that at the end of the year, when Poor Tithe was made, the farmer had stored grain and fruit out of which he could make Poor Tithe. Therefore, Poor Tithe in February-March, standing alone between the fruit and grain harvests, would be a manageable burden in the third and sixth years. I believe that in the third and sixth years the Israelite made First Tithe from each harvest (depending on what crops an individual farmer might sow), just as he always did. He made Festival Tithe in March-April, May-June, and September-October, as he did every year. In February-March (every third and sixth years), he also made Poor Tithe. The burden of the tithes was ten percent in any one month, making First, Festival, and Poor tithes manageable, reasonable, and economically feasible.

ASPECTS OF THE TITHES NOT GENERALLY RECOGNIZED

Five aspects of the four tithes are generally not recognized, or are overlooked.

- The priests did not tithe. Israel tithed to the Levites, the Levites tithed to the priests, the priests had no one to whom they might tithe. They were, literally, at the top of the food chain. As God's direct representatives they received the tithe in the place of God.
- First Tithe (and therefore Levites' Tithe) was not year-round, it was seasonal. Since First Tithe was made from the crop harvests, which took place mid-March through mid-November, and animals were (probably) tithed once a year after weaning (probably

May–July), then there was no First Tithe from mid-November through mid-March (compare 2 Chronicles 31:5–7).

- The Levites did not tithe from the lands which they possessed. The tribe of Levi did not have a portion of the land assigned to their tribe. The Levites were assigned certain cities within the territories of the other tribes as their dwelling place, and they possessed for their own use the lands immediately surrounding those cities, Numbers 35:1–8. Thus, the Levites could raise animals (and crops?) for their own use. However, they did not tithe from their own lands. They took a tithe from Israel (First Tithe) as wages for their service to attend to the needs of the priests and the tabernacle, Numbers 18:21–24, and made a tithe (Levites' Tithe) to the priests out of First Tithe.

- The Festival Tithe was made by, kept by, and used by the person making the tithe. The tither made a tithe to himself.

- If you were not a farmer, or you were poor, you had no obligation to tithe. Therefore, only part of the general population gave a tithe, or put another way, not everyone was required to tithe.[15]

WAS TITHING A LEGAL REQUIREMENT?

There are two types of laws. One type is casuistic law. Casuistic law expresses both the condition and the penalty, and is identified by an "If ... then" type of terminology. This type of law is sometimes known as "case law." For example, Exodus 21:20, "If a man beats his servant or his maidservant with a rod, so that he dies under his hand, he shall surely be punished."[16] The other kind of law is apodictic law. This is absolute law, stated in unconditional, categorical directives such as commands and prohibitions. For example, "honor your father and mother" and "you shall not murder."

---

15. Those who did not tithe supported the priests and temple through the sacrifices and offerings, and in other ways, Leviticus 27:1–29; Exodus 13:2; Numbers 18:15–16. Additionally, the common people provided the wood to burn the sacrifices on the altar (cf. Exodus 25:2, 5; Deuteronomy 29:11), and the oil for the lamps in the tabernacle (Exodus 27:20; 35:8, 14; Leviticus 24:2). In Jesus' time there was an annual festival of woodgathering in August to supply wood for the altar.

16. In some casuistic laws the punishment is implied, for example, Exodus 21:26–27.

The Tithe in Mosaic Times

The instructions concerning First Tithe, Numbers 18:21-24, were not expressed either as casuistic or apodictic law. Giving First Tithe was wholly voluntary. There was no civil or religious law, enforcement, or penalty to make people give First Tithe. For First Tithe there is no "You shall tithe," and there is no "If you do not tithe, then . . . [penalty]." First Tithe is identified as a heave offering, Numbers 18:24. As a heave offering, First Tithe was a part of the whole lifted up to the Lord in recognition that the whole belongs to the Lord and the part "heaved" belonged to the priests. The act of giving the tithe made it a heave offering, but nowhere in the Law are the children of Israel commanded to give First Tithe. As discussed below, the Levites were to "take" First Tithe, which does not mean to forcibly seize the tithe, but means to receive and take possession of First Tithe from the children of Israel. Therefore, giving First Tithe was wholly voluntary.[17]

The Levites' Tithe is expressed as apodictic law: "you shall offer up a heave offering [out of First Tithe] . . . a tithe of the tithes . . . you shall give the Lord's heave offering [the tithe of the tithes] to Aaron."[18] Festival Tithe was apodictic law, Deuteronomy 14:22, "you shall tithe a tithe [of] all the increase of your grain that the field produces year by year." Poor Tithe was apodictic law, 14:28, "at the end of every third year you shall bring out the tithe . . . and store it within your gates." Deuteronomy 26:13 makes clear that Poor Tithe was a Law, "I have not transgressed your commandments" concerning the Poor Tithe in v. 12. First Tithe, then, was a religious and moral obligation, but not a legal requirement. The Levites' tithe to the priests, and the Festival and Poor Tithes, were required, but no specific punishment was stated for failure to tithe.

---

17. Since it was First Tithe that was used to support the religious system (as support for Levites and priests) its voluntary nature has implications for Christian giving. For example, I have attended churches where those who did not give ten percent of their income could not serve in a church ministry. Such a rule is completely contrary to the voluntary nature of First Tithe. Christianity conducted according to Scripture principles recognizes the voluntary nature of giving to support church ministers and ministries, and does not punish poor believers by denying them a place to serve Christ.

18. There is no people group in the New Testament church corresponding to the Levites—every New Testament believer is a priest. Therefore, the apodictic law of the Levites' Tithe has no influence on Christian giving. The same is true of the Festival Tithe, as there are no mandatory festivals in Christianity, although there are principles that may be drawn from Festival Tithe to guide New Testament giving. The same is true of Poor Tithe. There is no New Testament law requiring one to support the poor, but there are Old and New Testament principles to encourage and guide such giving.

In light of the above discussion, it is interesting to note that tithes are not specifically mentioned in the "blessings and cursing" sections of the Law, Leviticus 26; Deuteronomy 27–31. The commandments that are to be obeyed for blessing, Leviticus 26:1–4, are essentially a recapitulation of commandments one through four in the Ten Commandments. Obedience will result in the land yielding its produce; disobedience will result in the land not yielding its produce. The tithe is not mentioned, although obviously obedience will result in larger tithes. The quite specific curses in Deuteronomy 27:1–26 have nothing to do with the tithe, nor do the blessings that follow in chapter 28. Tithing was not part of the covenant between God and Israel. By this I mean that tithing did not require God to bless his people, and failure to tithe did not require him to curse his people, under the terms and conditions in Leviticus 26 and Deuteronomy 27–31. As a matter of faithfulness or faithlessness, tithing affected the relationship the people had with YHWH. This is true of every believer's relationship with God. A life of righteousness, which is a life of worship, fellowship, obedience, and service to God, results in blessing. A life of disobedience, which draws the believer away from worship, fellowship, and service, results in a lack of blessing, and chastisement. Maintenance of the Mosaic covenant, however, did not depend on the tithe, except in that general way that righteousness versus disobedience has toward all of God's commandments. The divine law in operation concerning the tithe is the moral law of sowing and reaping. If the tither gave as God had commanded, then God would give as he had promised. When the tithe was practiced it resulted in personal blessing to the tither; when ignored it resulted in a lack of blessing to the person. The same may be said of the righteous works required of the non-tithing population.

HOW WAS THE TITHE GIVEN?

God did not give Israel any rules or guidance as to the manner of giving and disbursing the tithes. Many commentators assume First Tithe was always brought to the tabernacle (later the temple) for disbursement to the Levites. Since First Tithe was a heave offering an argument might be made for collection at and disbursement from the tabernacle-temple. However, one might also argue that the act of giving the tithe made First Tithe a heave offering: the tithe, being a holy thing, was in effect lifted up to the Lord when it was given to the Levite. Pragmatic reality probably trumped other considerations, and I believe First Tithe was given at or near to the places the Levites lived.

During the wilderness-wandering years it would have been a reasonable practice to give First Tithe at the tabernacle. However, after Israel conquered the land, and the tribes spread out into their lands and cities, and the population grew, the key issues in giving First Tithe would have been transportation and storage. We must forget modern means of transportation and think only of foot travel, wooden carts, dirt paths, and donkeys. The same is true of storage—we must forget about modern silos and methods of preservation. Grains, fruits (or wine and oil), and nuts have a certain weight by volume, and a certain bulk, which set limits to then-current means of transportation and storage. A harvest (minus First Tithe) might be sold to a merchant a little at a time because the farmer would be better equipped than the merchant to store the whole harvest. Farms were close by the cities, so city people might have bought directly from the farmer, or perhaps at the ancient equivalent of a "Farmers' Market." Sheep, goats, cattle, and oxen must be walked to the place of sale, or sold a few at a time and walked by the buyer to home, or by the merchant to market. These same issues were also problems to be solved for giving and receiving First Tithe. There are several good solutions to the problem. First Tithe might have been given by the individual farmer to individual Levites. It may have been brought to a nearby city and disbursed to the Levites living in the area. Or, First Tithe might have been brought to a nearby Levitical city, which were scattered throughout Israel, and disbursed to Levites living in those cities. Certainly the "long journey" provision for Festival Tithe provides guidance: there was no provision to turn First Tithe into money, thus making a long journey unlikely for First Tithe. Because of the transportation problems involved with the weight and volume of the agricultural product, and the equally problematic transportation of animals, it seems unlikely to me that all Israel brought First Tithe to the Jerusalem Temple, where storage would add an additional problem, until the time of Hezekiah, 2 Chronicles 31:5–12.[19] The more plausible solution is that the farmer brought First Tithe to the Levitical cities, where it was received and distributed by the Levites and priests.

---

19. Hezekiah caused rooms in the temple complex to be used as storerooms for the tithes. However, and more to the point of the current discussion, Hezekiah's kingdom consisted of the tribes of Judah and Benjamin, so the volume of tithes to be stored was much smaller than in the days when Israel consisted of twelve tribes.

Scripture also does not state how the grains, fruits, and nuts were to be measured or counted for the purpose of tithing. The most reasonable solution is that these items were tithed according to volume. In modern terms, the tithe on ten bushels of wheat would be one bushel.

The Levites were to "take" First Tithe, Numbers 18:26. The word translated "take" is the Hebrew *laqah*. This word has many nuances of meaning, but the best meaning here is "to take possession of."[20] This does not mean the Levites seized the tithe, but that they received it and took possession of it. This word is translated "receive" in v. 28, "you [Levites] shall also offer a heave offering [the Levites' Tithe] to the Lord from all your tithes which you receive [*laqah*] from the children of Israel." First Tithe was received, *laqah*, from Israel by the Levites, who took possession of it, *laqah*, in the act of receiving the tithe. The idea behind receiving the tithe and taking the tithe is a transfer of ownership or responsibility. Once First Tithe had been given the farmer's responsibility had been fulfilled. Proper use of that tithe became the Levites' responsibility. A friendly relationship is in view. The Levites lived among the tribes in forty-eight cities scattered throughout Israel. The tithes they received were given to them by their neighbors, whom they lived with, and on whose behalf they ministered to the Lord in the tabernacle. First Tithe was to be given and received as a mutually beneficial relationship between brethren.

The Levites' Tithe to the priests was apparently to be given in a similar manner, that is, by individual Levites to priests living in the same area or city. The manner of presentation is not specified, which most likely means the priests were to wait for the Levites to give them the tithe. When the instruction at Numbers 18:28 was written the only priests were Aaron and his sons. However, as Aaron's family increased, the name "Aaron" came to identify all the priests. During the time of King David the priests were so numerous that they were organized into twenty-four groups, and each group was assigned specific dates to serve in the temple (one week, twice each year, plus during each festival). Under these circumstances it is reasonable to assume the Levites' Tithe was directly given from Levite to priest. Again, centralized locations for disbursement are probable. It is not impossible that in later times the Levites took their tithe to the

---

20. Harris et al., *Wordbook*, 1:481; Wilson, *Word Studies*, 441; *Gesenius' Lexicon*, 434.

The Tithe in Mosaic Times

temple, from where it was equitably distributed to the priests, perhaps during their temple service rotation.[21]

WHEN WAS THE AGRICULTURAL PRODUCT TITHED?

When Were the Food Crops Tithed?

Since First Tithe and Festival Tithe included food crops, giving these tithes was probably arranged according to the various harvests.[22] Various grains, fruits, and nuts ripened at different times throughout the year. Nominally the harvest began about mid-March and ended about mid-November. Borowski[23] describes the harvest cycle from the settlement of the land (circa 1400 BC) to the destruction of the first temple (586 BC):

	April	May	June	July	Aug	Sep	Oct	Nov
Wheat		X						
Barley	X							
Oats			X					
Peas		X	X					
Chickpeas				X				
Lentils		X	X					
Vetch		X	X					
Sesame				X				
Flax				X				
Millet				X	X			
Grapes			X	X	X	X		
Figs					X	X		
Pomegranates					X	X		
Olives						X	X	X

The festival cycle paralleled the harvest cycle (Purim, Woodgathering, and Dedication were added after the Babylonian Captivity).

---

21. During the divided kingdom and after the Babylonian Captivity First Tithe was brought to the temple, 2 Chronicles 31; Nehemiah 10, 12.
22. Poor Tithe was given at the end of the year, between harvests. Levites' Tithe was probably given periodically, that is, as the Levites received First Tithe.
23. Borowski, *Agriculture in Iron Age Israel*, 37.

- Purim (Esther 9:18ff), February–March (13 Adar)
- Passover-Unleavened Bread (Leviticus 23), March–April (14 Nisan)
- Pentecost (Leviticus 23) in May–June (Sivan), 50 days after Passover
- Woodgathering (Nehemiah 10:34), August (15 Av, also known as Ab)
- Trumpets (Leviticus 23), September–October (first day of Tishri)
- Day of Atonement (Leviticus 23), September–October (ten days after Trumpets)
- Tabernacles (Leviticus 23), in September–October (five days after Atonement)
- Dedication (or Lights), in November–December (25th Kislev)

The beginning of the barley harvest corresponded to Passover-Unleavened Bread, the beginning of the wheat harvest to Pentecost, and the fruit harvest to Tabernacles. First Tithe would respond to the harvest cycles, as would the Levites' Tithe. Festival Tithe occurred three times a year because timed with the harvests associated with the mandatory festivals. Poor Tithe was between the harvests every third and sixth year in February–March. All the tithes, then, "of the seed of the land or of the fruit of the tree," were given and received throughout the year.[24]

First Tithe on food crops could be made in any, perhaps every month from April through November, depending on the crop a farmer had sown (grain) or planted (vines, fruit/nut trees). The Levites' Tithe could be made in every month in which they received First Tithe. The persons receiving these tithes did not have to provide for immense storage. Rather, these tithes came in throughout the year in a quantity manageable for transportation, storage, and daily use by the individuals receiving them. Poor Tithe in the third and sixth years was made in February–March out

---

24. Again, in my view transportation would be the driving force behind tithing throughout the year versus an annual tithe. This does not mean a small farm might not consolidate several small harvests into First Tithe, but the Law, since it did not specify when or how, was flexible enough to allow for a reasonable and individual approach to First Tithe.

of the remainder of the harvest. Grain, fruits, and nuts were harvested and stored by the farmer throughout the year, but out of that stored produce the farmer sold some and used some for himself. When Poor Tithe was made it was ten percent of what remained of the farmer's reduced stock of grain, fruit, and nuts. Therefore, the amount of Poor Tithe given to the cities to store for the needs of their poor was of a manageable quantity.

When Were the Animals Tithed?

Animals were tithed only in First Tithe and Festival Tithe. When was the animal tithe taken for First Tithe? Three schemes are plausible based on the conception-to-weaning cycle of the herds and flocks.[25] The first is a tithe just prior to the birthing season. However, under this scheme the Levites would have been responsible for managing the birth of any pregnant tithed animal. The second scheme would be to tithe the animals at the mandatory festivals, requiring three animal tithes throughout the year. This seems an unfair burden to the farmer, who would lose valuable stock three times a year. Additionally, herding animals to Jerusalem for First Tithe would be contrary to the long-journey provision made for Festival Tithe (there was no provision to convert First Tithe animals to money—which would need to be reconverted to animals upon arrival at Jerusalem, because money was not used as a tithe. There would soon be more money to be converted than animals to buy.) The most likely scheme for tithing animals for First Tithe was after newborns were weaned.[26] This would place the burden of husbandry on the farmer. The farmer would suffer less loss of his mature ewes because the newly weaned animals would form part of the total count from which the tithe was taken. The Levites would be more likely to receive animals that had the best chances of survival.

---

25. Sheep and goats give birth once or twice a year. The sexual season for sheep and goats runs from January to July, and gestation is about 150 days. Weaning is done when the lambs or kids are fifty to sixty days old. Cattle and oxen calve once a year. Cattle have a gestation period of nine months, oxen eight and one-half months. Calves are weaned when seven to eight months old.

26. Keil and Delitszch, *Commentary*, 1:645, say "the additions to the flock and herd were tithed" and remark that this was the "correct" interpretation of the Rabbins. This interpretation is based on a misapplication of Deuteronomy 12:6–7, 17–18; 14:22 to First Tithe. I understand Leviticus 27:31 as indicating the entire herd or flock was to pass under the rod for First Tithe. The "understanding" of the Rabbins seems calculated to ensure they never received any old, maimed, or sick sheep. God, who is no respecter of persons, did not punish the farmer in this manner, nor so favor the priests.

Moreover, a tithe after weaning corresponds by analogy to a tithe after each harvest. If the animal tithe for First Tithe took place once a year, then a tithe between May–July is consistent with the "after weaning" view.

The farmer was required to take a tithe of the animals three times a year for Festival Tithe. Deuteronomy 12:6–7, 17–18; 14:22 requires the animal tithe for Festival Tithe be from the firstlings of the herd and flock. This seems counterintuitive for two reasons. One, it required the farmer to keep track of which animals were the firstborn. However, the farmer must keep track of the firstborn for sacrificial purposes, both for his own sins and to sell firstborn animals to others. Second, the firstborn were the future of the herd and flock, so it would seem that tithing the firstborn would hurt the farmer. However, a tithe taken from only the firstborn reduced the number of animals subject to Festival Tithe, thus reducing the tithe, versus a tithe from the whole herd or flock. Since this tithe was taken three times a year that reduction was significant. One must also consider that these animals, unless the tithe was converted to money, must be walked to Jerusalem. Fewer animals meant less transportation problems for the farmer.

WHAT WAS THE EFFECT OF THE SABBATH CYCLE ON THE TITHES?

The four tithes were affected by the seven-year Sabbath cycle, Leviticus 25:1–7, 18–22. This seven year cycle was used to regulate food crop production (and served as a test of faith). In the seventh year the arable land was to lay fallow—no sowing or harvesting. Whatever grew naturally, from sowing in previous years, and from seed that had inadvertently fallen during previous harvests, was to be allowed to grow naturally. The farmer was prohibited from harvesting his land. All persons (including the farmer) and all animals were allowed to enter the fallow lands and collect food for their daily sustenance. God also promised that in exchange for their faithfulness the land would produce more crops in the sixth year. The following table shows the relationship between the Sabbath year cycle and the tithes.

The Tithe in Mosaic Times

Year	Harvests	Tithe
One	Sow and Harvest	First, Levites', Festival
Two	Sow and Harvest	First, Levites', Festival
Three	Sow and Harvest	First, Levites', Festival, Poor
Four	Sow and Harvest	First, Levites', Festival
Five	Sow and Harvest	First, Levites', Festival
Six	Sow and Harvest. Sufficient for three years	First, Levites', Festival and Poor
Seven	Fields Fallow	No Harvest = No food crop tithes. Animal tithes would be required

The Poor Tithe had a definite relation with the Sabbath year cycle. God promised to make year six so bountiful the food crops from the sixth year would last for three years (Leviticus 25:21), meaning years seven, one, and two of the cycle. The poor could glean extra grain in the sixth year. The Poor Tithe stored in the cities for their poor would be greater in the sixth year, thus preparing the cities for the leaner seventh year of the Sabbath cycle. In the seventh year the poor could glean without restriction, but the natural production of the fallow land would not yield the same quantity as when seed was sown, and in the seventh year everyone, and every animal, became a gleaner, thus increasing competition for the grain. However, the poor would be helped by the Poor Tithe stored from year six. In the first year of the cycle, when the harvests might be smaller, or farmers less willing to let the poor glean, the poor could still be helped by the Poor Tithe stored from the bountiful sixth year. As the Sabbath cycle continued the Poor Tithe given in year three would replenish the depleted food stocks stored in the cities, and thereby help the poor in years four and five. In year six the bountiful harvest gave the poor greater opportunities for gleaning, and the Poor Tithe would replenish the stores of food in preparation for the fallow seventh year.

A BRIEF SUMMARY

The economy of ancient Israel was predominantly agricultural in nature. No money, no precious metals, and no non-agricultural products were given as a tithe. Food crops and animals were tithed in First Tithe and Festival Tithe. Only food crops were tithed in Levites' Tithe and Poor

Tithe. Scripture does not tell us the unit of measurement for the food crop tithes, but it was probably measured in units of volume, for example, one bushel of wheat tithed for every ten bushels reaped. The following question-answer statements briefly define Israel's tithes.

- What was the theological basis of the tithe? The land was wholly owned by YHWH, therefore the product of the land belonged to YHWH. In one sense, Israel was a tenant who owed a portion of the land's product to the Owner. In a secondary but equal sense, Israel acknowledged God's blessings by returning a token of their blessing to him. The tithe helped support the nation's religious structure, the worshiper, and the poor.
- What was tithed? The agricultural product of the land: grains, fruits, nuts, cattle, oxen, sheep, goats.
- How many tithes? Four tithes: First Tithe, Levites' Tithe, Festival Tithe, and Poor Tithe.
- Who received the four tithes? First Tithe was made by Israel to the Levites. Levites' Tithe was made by the Levites to the priests out of First Tithe. Festival Tithe was made three times a year by the farmer to himself for his use at the three mandatory festivals. Poor Tithe was given by the farmer to his local city in years three and six (of the Sabbath cycle) for distribution to the poor.
- Why did the priests receive a tithe? Because they were the direct representatives of God to the people. The tithe was owed to the Lord; the priests received the tithe on behalf of the Lord. This is why First Tithe and Levites' Tithe were heave offerings.
- Why didn't the priests tithe? Positionally they represented God, the tithe belonged to God, and they received the tithe on behalf of God.
- Why did the Levites receive a tithe? As payment for their full time service to meet the needs of the temple and the priests.
- Why did the poor receive a tithe? As part of God's welfare system for the poor.
- Why did the farmer tithe to himself (Festival Tithe)? So he would have the means to attend the three festivals and enjoy his time of worship.

The Tithe in Mosaic Times

- How much was tithed? First Tithe: 10% of the grains, fruits, and nuts, and 10% of the animals. Levites' Tithe: 10% out of the grains, fruits, and nuts received in First Tithe. Festival Tithe: 10% of the grains, fruits, or nuts according to the harvest corresponding to the festival, and 10% of animals (firstlings only). Poor Tithe: 10% of the grains, fruits, and nuts remaining in the farmer's storage at the end of years three and six of the Sabbath cycle.

- What was the total burden of the tithes. The tithe burden for the Levites was ten percent out of First Tithe. The burden for the farmer seems to be twenty-seven percent (First+Festival+Poor=27%). However, the tithe burden was only ten percent in five of the eight months of harvest. In the other three months the farmer gave Festival Tithe, which increased the tithe burden to nineteen percent. However, all of Festival Tithe belonged to the farmer, who would have eaten it or sold it under other circumstances, so Festival Tithe was not a loss to the farmer, and the tithe burden was the ten percent of First Tithe. From November through March no tithes were made, except the ten percent Poor Tithe in the third and sixth years. In every practical way the tithe burden to the farmer was never more than ten percent.

- When were the tithes made? First Tithe: food crops after each harvest; animals once a year after weaning. Levites Tithe: after receiving First Tithe. Festival Tithe: at the harvest appropriate to the festival. Poor Tithe was made at the end of years three and six of the Sabbath cycle.

- Where were the tithes given? First Tithe and Levites' Tithe were probably taken to a nearby Levitical city (in later history to the temple). The Festival Tithe was made at the farmer's home and taken by him to the festivals. The Poor Tithe was made by the farmer at his own village.

- Could a tithe be "bought back" from the Lord? First Tithe grains, fruits, and nuts could be redeemed for their value plus one-fifth. The redemption money was not a tithe but was given in lieu of that tithe. Animals could not be redeemed.

- Was tithing year-round? No tithe was made mid-November through mid-March.

- Were there times when the tithe was not given? If there was no food crop harvest, such as in the seventh "Sabbatical" year, or because severe drought, locusts, or disease had destroyed a food crop, then there was no food crop with which to make a tithe.
- Were there some who did not tithe? Yes, the priests, the poor, non-farmers, the foreigner living in the land. The tithe was the agricultural product of the land. If you were not producing grains, fruits, nuts, herds, or flocks you had nothing to tithe. Money was not tithed.

THE PURPOSE OF THE MOSAIC TITHE

What Was the Religious Purpose?

Every offering was holy to the Lord, so the heave offering was made out of the holy things which the children of Israel offered to the Lord, Numbers 18:19. First and Levites' Tithe were heave offerings to the Lord that were given to the Levites and the priests. These supported the Levites and priests as full time ministry professionals. A "heave offering" is the Hebrew word *t^eruma*. Although movement is implied by the translation, the term simply meant a gift or offering. The heave offering was: the thigh of the ram of consecration, Exodus 29:27; the thigh of the animal sacrifice and a cake of blended flour and oil from the peace offering, Leviticus 7:14; the thigh of the peace offering when completing a Nazirite vow, Numbers 6:20; a cake of ground meal in celebration of the harvest of the land, Numbers 15:19; First Tithe and Levites' Tithe, Numbers 18:24, 26; spoils from the war with the Midianites, Numbers 31:41. In relation to the animal and grain sacrifices made at the altar, the heave offering indicated that a part of the sacrifice belonged to the priest as his food. The same was true of the tithe. By identifying the tithe as a heave offering a statement was made that the tithe belonged to YHWH and was given to the priest by YHWH.[27]

Festival Tithe provided the means wherein the tither could joyously celebrate the festivals of the Lord. These festivals celebrated salvation, the firstfruits of the harvest, and the fullness of the harvest, Exodus 23:15–16. Poor Tithe is pronounced as "holy," Deuteronomy 26:13, giving it a religious character.

---

27. Kurtz, *Sacrificial Worship*, 269.

The Tithe in Mosaic Times

The tithe was a recognition that the whole harvest belonged to the Lord. The believer acknowledged God's blessings by giving to God a portion of those very blessings. The Sabbath year supported the view that the whole product of the land was the Lord's by giving all the natural product of the land to all the people and animals: the Lord does what he wants with his own. What might have been a tithe in the seventh, Sabbath, year was returned to the people as a blessing for their faith in prior years. Giving to God was not some spiritual or intangible exercise. Through the tithe God provided a way for his people to tangibly understand that their God was real and was an active participant in their lives.

What Were the Civil Purposes?

The tithes served three civil purposes. The first was to support the people who served in the religious system. The tribe of Levi was not assigned territory in the promised land. They were given forty-eight cities as their dwelling place. A land area around the cities belonged to Levi for pasturage (and possibly gardens?), Numbers 35:1–8.[28] This small amount of land may or may not have been a reliable supply of food, depending on how many people occupied the city and used the land. The tribe, then, required a larger, more dependable, and constant source of food. The Levites had no part in the sacrifices and offerings. Their primary food source was First Tithe. The priests retained certain parts of the animal and grain sacrifices and offerings for their food, but this was hardly sufficient to support them and their families year-round. The Levites' Tithe was their primary food source.

The second civil use was to support the theocratic form of government. In the centuries before the kings the priests were the arbiters of civil law. Between the giving of the Law and the time of the kings the tithes supported the civil government as well as the religious establishment.[29]

---

28. Numbers 35:4, 5 seem contradictory but are not. The most reasonable solution is that the thousand cubits, v. 4, is the depth of the land outward from the city wall, and the two thousand cubits is the width of the land running alongside the side of the city. See Budd, *Numbers*, 376. Assuming an eighteen inch cubit, the land area on each side of the wall would be 3,000 feet wide and 1,500 feet deep.

29. The judges were not civil governors but more in the line of patriots used by YHWH to motivate the people to repentance and to help them overcome their Gentile oppressors. The judges appear to have worked in one or more tribal territories. Only Samuel appears to have judged the whole of Israel.

The third civil purpose of the tithe was to help the poor as part of the welfare system. God clearly stated that Israel had a continuing civic responsibility to help the poor, Deuteronomy 15:7–11. The Law concerning gleaning, Leviticus 19:10–11; Deuteronomy 24:19–22, was only part of God's welfare plan. Gleaning allowed the poor the dignity of earning their daily sustenance. The Poor Tithe supplemented their gleaning and sustained them during the four months between the end of one harvest season and the beginning of the next. The Poor Tithe assisted the poor during the seven year Sabbath cycle for the arable land. The increased crops during year six increased the tithe at the end of year six, thereby increasing the food supplies stocked in the cities for their poor. This helped the poor during years seven, one, and two of the Sabbath cycle. At the end of year three Poor Tithe replenished those depleted stocks. Thus, the complete welfare system for the poor was a combination of self-employment (gleaning) and food given to them by their city government.

What Was the Moral Purpose?

The tithes served a moral purpose. The four tithes established a bond between brethren. Through First Tithe the Israelite provided for his religious brethren: the priests who ministered on their behalf as mediators between God and his people; the Levites who serviced the needs of priests and temple. Festival Tithes allowed and encouraged all Israel to worship publically as one congregation. Poor Tithe made the common man his brother's keeper, and gave the poor man a reason to bless God and his charitable brother. The greatest blessing of the tithes was that they established a sense of community; they bound one to another in a mutually beneficial symbiosis. Through tithing and gleaning bonds of friendship and community could develop between giver and receiver.

LEVI AND THE TITHE

Why Did Levi Receive a Tithe as His Inheritance?

First Tithe was given to the tribe of Levi as their inheritance in the land, Numbers 18:21, "I have given the children of Levi all the tithes in Israel as an inheritance in return for the work which they perform, the work of the tabernacle of meeting." The part of First Tithe that went to the Levites was given them as wages for their service to the priests and temple, Numbers

18:6, and their service to the people, 18:22–23. The priests received tithes as wages for their work, and as God's representatives, 18:8, 11, 19. Why did the tribe of Levi receive tithes instead of land as their inheritance?

In Genesis 49 the dying Jacob blessed his sons. His "blessing" to Simeon and Levi was especially cruel.

> Genesis 49:5-7, "Simeon and Levi are brothers; instruments of cruelty are in their dwelling place. Let not my soul enter their council; let not my honor be united to their assembly; for in their anger they slew a man, and in their self-will they hamstrung an ox. Cursed be their anger, for it is fierce; and their wrath, for it is cruel! I will divide them in Jacob and scatter them in Israel."

Simeon's problems do not concern this discussion. God did scatter Levi in Israel, in forty-eight cities within territories belonging to the other tribes. Jacob cursed his son's anger and wrath. Is it coincidence that Levi bore the wrath of God for the rest of Israel, Numbers 18:1, 5, 7? Jacob disinherited Levi and Simeon, "let not my soul enter their council; let not my honor be united to their assembly." Levi had no inheritance in the land, Numbers 18:20.

God's ways are not our ways. The tribe from the man who unjustly killed others (Genesis 34), find their life path in redeeming sinner's worthy of death, by offering death in the place of the sinner: by sacrificing animals on behalf of other men who are themselves sinners worthy of death. Levi's meat is the fruit of his life: parts from the bodies of the animals he sacrifices, remains from the fruit and grains he offers. His disinherited state causes him to be a burden to his brethren, living on their tithes, sacrifices, and offerings. On the other hand, God turned Jacob's curse into a blessing. Levi ministers on behalf of his brethren, receiving tithes from them as his inheritance and wages, Numbers 18:21. God raised Levi out of the dark pit of Jacob's anger to become the mediators of the covenant and the spiritual types of the deliverance Jesus was to bring. They were the mediators between God and man, they administered God's grace and mercy, they restored sinners to fellowship with God, they demonstrated the blessings of serving the one true God, and they were living illustrations of the love, grace, and truth of God in the Christ who was to come.

Why Did Levi Receive Tithes?

Levi received tithes because God is a just God. Justice requires men receive what is due from their works. Levi labored in the temple and received a wage for his labor. Levi's wage was the tithe, Numbers 18:8, 21. If Levi faithfully served the Lord, then his brethren would be informed as to God's Laws and blessed by growth in spiritual maturity. Their growth in grace would in turn lead Israel to be faithful to all the Law, including the instructions concerning the tithes. The closer Levi brought Israel into fellowship with God, the more Levi would receive the blessing for his works. Therefore, Levi's burden was threefold. One, he must serve the Lord as commanded, maintaining the nation's fellowship with YHWH. Second, he was to teach and encourage Israel to walk in obedience to the Lord. Third he was to provide the means by which fellowship could be restored after an act of disobedience.

The tithes established Levi as truly set apart to serve God on behalf of their brethren. Levi labored for none but God, earned wages from no other, owed no other allegiance, and served God's interests only. The tithe was the Lord's, as to its origin and source. That the tithe was routed to Levi through their brethren created moral and civil bonds between the people and their ministers, but it did not change the fact that the tithe was the Lord's. Thus, Levi was freed from all burdens other than the one burden of serving God in every capacity demanded of Levi by the Law.

The tithes established Levi as the servant of the people of Israel. Levi labored on behalf of all Israel. Levi served the Lord in the place of the other tribes. He earned his wages by serving as the mediator for his brethren. His brethren justly owed Levi for this service. The tithe helped establish Levi's allegiance to the spiritual welfare of the people. By taking a tithe from his brethren Levi placed himself in the position of servant and teacher to his brothers and sisters in the Lord.

THE TITHE AND THE ECONOMY

What Was the Effect of the Tithe on Israel's Economy?

The tithe, if properly given and used, would have stabilized the agricultural economy by acting against the root causes of inflation and recession. Inflation occurs when there is less product than there is money. The value of the product rises according to an increased demand for less available

The Tithe in Mosaic Times

product. Because more money is required to buy less product, the value of money in relation to product falls, which is inflation: it takes more money to buy the product. Recession occurs when there is more product than there is money. Production falls, people are out of work, a recession occurs. The cycle is: too much product in relation to money, demand falls, therefore production falls, resulting in a shortage of the product, which leads to inflation, rising prices, less production, and recession. The changing fortunes of the product is called supply and demand.

In Israel the tithe affected both supply and demand for the basic product of an agricultural society: food. First and Festival Tithes affected supply by diverting up to nineteen percent of production away from the market. The tithe affected demand by providing agricultural products to two large user groups: the tribe of Levi and the poor. By diverting excess production to these two consumer groups the tithe had a positive effect on the internal causes of inflation and recession.

The tithe also controlled the potentially disruptive effects of the thrice yearly festivals. If all those celebrating the festivals—potentially every male in Israel—were required to buy all their food at Jerusalem, the sudden demand on the economy would have caused sharply rising prices.[30] Production, transportation, and marketing would have adapted to respond to a sharply rising demand three times a year, resulting in a disproportionate amount of the planting devoted to satisfying the demand. After the festival demand would have sharply dropped, encouraging recession. Just before the festivals demand would sharply rise producing inflation. The economy would have literally been a cycle of feast and famine.[31] Unstable prices lead to an unstable economy.

Another benefit of the tithe is that it did not remove money from the economy. There was little incentive to redeem a tithe. More pertinent, if the tithe had been money, too much money would have been concentrated in the hands of a few people: the tribe of Levi. Less money would have been available to the population as a whole. Less money in circulation results in recession, perhaps leading to economic depression. The result would have been devastating to religion. The Levites would have become bankers providing credit to the other tribes. Moreover, the Levites would

---

30. Only those who had a long journey could convert their Festival Tithe into money, to be reconverted to food at Jerusalem.

31. Compare the American economy's response to the Thanksgiving-Christmas cycle.

have flooded the economy with their money to buy food. Large spending by one people group on a few crucial items would have led to higher prices, less product, and economic instability.

The tithe also relieved the populace from the heavy taxation required to support a welfare system. The most basic need of the poor was met by their work at gleaning and the Poor Tithe. Money could be spent on housing and other necessities instead of food. The tithe also supported the limited needs of the very limited government. Israel was in effect self-governing. Tribal elders decided most issues, and the most difficult legal cases were decided by the priests. When Israel demanded a king, they were warned that, in addition to their tithe, their new government would require ten percent of their agricultural product for its support, 1 Samuel 8:15, 17.

Why Wasn't Money Tithed?

In addition to the above, a tithe of money would have turned Israel to a credit-debit economy funded by wealthy banks owned by the Levites and priests. In ancient Israel money was primarily lent by friends and family. There were, of course, money lenders, but the Law strictly regulated the finance charges (usury). Money circulates from buyers to sellers to bankers, where it is sold back to buyers as credit—a loan—which costs more to pay back (finance charges and other fees) than the original value. A tithe of food takes care of itself by disappearing into the population and reviving demand, which affects production. The demand for food is self-regulating: people constantly consume, only so much can be stored, so there is a steady demand on production. A predictable demand results in a steady production that stabilizes the economy.

If the tithe was money,[32] then the farmer would have to find sufficient buyers for his product to satisfy the demand for a money tithe. The Levites and priests would in turn have to take that money to buy their food from the market place, which would have increased in value because the re-seller needed to make a profit. The increased demand at

---

32. In later times the Jews recognized the destabilizing effects of money as a tithe. Limits were placed on redeeming a tithe. The redemption money could not be of one currency, for example, not all silver or copper coins, but the entire amount must be made up of mixed currencies, to avoid raising the prices of copper and silver, Mishna, *Maaser Sheni*, 2.7–2.9. If the population had come to Jerusalem during the festivals with one currency, then the monetary exchange would have destabilized the economy.

The Tithe in Mosaic Times

higher prices would have resulted in less product and rising prices. In an agricultural economy buyers and sellers are in short demand because most people grow their own crops and raise their own animals. In an agricultural economy the most demand for product comes from the non-agrarian population, which is small compared to the agrarian population, and from those farmers who specialize in some one product (for example, grapes for wine.[33])

WHY DIDN'T THE NON-AGRARIAN POPULACE TITHE?

Since the tithe was of the seed of the land, of the fruit of the tree, and the herds and flocks, I have made an assumption that only those growing crops or raising animals were required to tithe. However, one might make a case that the non-agrarian populace tithed on what they bought at market (or direct from the farmer). Nothing in the Law prohibited this practice, but nothing in the Law required the non-agrarian populace to tithe. The Pharisees in Jesus' time thought they needed to tithe on food they had bought (Matthew 23:23). Certainly one might make First Tithe in this manner, although the amount tithed would by necessity be exceedingly small.[34] However, the tithe is "of the land" and "of the tree" and "of the herd or the flock." These words indicate agricultural production, not agricultural product obtained from the marketplace. The farmer and the husbandman tithed from the product of their labor. The buyer neither farmed nor ranched, so what he purchased was not the labor of his hands, and therefore he did not owe a tithe. Obviously the Law did not subject the poor to a tithe.[35] Since the poor did not own any fields from which

---

33. Agrarian specialization in a money-driven economy is also destabilizing. "In New Testament times Rome's insatiable appetites and seductive wealth lured provincials with money to invest in what they could export to Rome, rather than the needs of their people. Landowners in Asia used so much land for export items like wine that Asia's cities had to import grain from Egypt to the south or from the Black Sea area to the north; the landowners profited, but everyone else paid higher prices for basic food needs," Keener, *Revelation*, 427.

34. Later Judaism, Mishnah, *Maaseroth*, 2.1, taught that what people brought into their houses was subject to tithe. Even what the ants stole was subject to tithe, *Maaseroth*, 5.7.

35. Later Judaism did not tithe the gleaner, but did sometimes require the owner to tithe on what had been gleaned, especially if the gleanings came from a field owned by a Gentile, Mishnah, *Peah*, 6.1, and other applicable passages.

agricultural product could be tithed, Deuteronomy 14:22, then they could not be subject to any tithe.

The tithe came from the labors of the farmer. As noted earlier, the non-agrarian population had several non-tithing means to meet their religious, civil, and moral responsibilities. All were required to help the poor. The poor needed more than food, they needed shelter, clothing, and other sundries that support daily living. The non-agrarian population could give money to the poor. They could contribute wood and oil to the temple, and money for charitable giving.[36] Although later Judaism required everyone to tithe something, even the priests, this was not God's intent, as clearly demonstrated in the instructions God gave for tithing.

SUMMARY OF THE MOSAIC LAW CONCERNING THE TITHE

We are used to thinking of what remains after giving as "less than what I had." It is far more productive to think of that remainder as "the Lord is providing all that I need." The priests lived on ten percent of the food crops out of the First Tithe, plus meat, grain, and oil from the sacrifices and offerings made at the altar, and what they might raise or grow in a little plot of land attached to their city of residence. The Levites lived on the ninety percent they kept from First Tithe, plus what they could produce on their own lands surrounding the Levitical cities. The tithe the Levites and priests received was what God deemed sufficient. So it was also with the farmer. Obviously the farmer continued to prosper after tithing (else agriculture and tithing would have ceased) proving that these tithes did not impair the farmer's ability to provide for himself and his family. What remained after the First, Festival, and Poor Tithes was the Lord providing all their needs. Agricultural production always exceeded the tithes, and for all but the smallest farmer, exceeded their personal needs; otherwise the non-agrarian population would have starved. The tithers had grain, fruit, nuts, and animals enough to sell as well as tithe. What they sold re-

---

36. Edersheim, *Life and Times*, 2:387, describes charitable giving in the time of Jesus from Luke 21:2. Along the colonnades in the Court of the Women were thirteen "trumpets," (funnels) that lead to chambers used to collect charitable giving. Each "trumpet" had an inscription "marking the objects of contributions—whether to make up for past neglect, to pay for certain sacrifices, to provide incense, wood, or for other gifts." There were also trumpets for "gifts to be distributed in secret to the children of the pious poor."

sulted in money to buy other products to meet their needs. God, through the tithe, took care of the basic necessities of all his people.

Only the agrarian populace tithed. If they failed to tithe the tribe of Levi must respond by teaching and preaching the Word of the Lord concerning the congregation's religious, civil, and moral obligations. Levi's dependence on the tithe gave them an incentive to perform their duties with passion, interest, and professionalism. A people desiring spirituality had an interest in supporting Levi. This mutual concern for each other's welfare, so clearly illustrated in the tithe, formed the basis for Israel's religion: love God and love your neighbor as yourself.

THE TITHE FROM JOSHUA TO THE GOSPELS

Perhaps the first discussion should be why I have placed the gospels in the chapter on the tithe in Mosaic times. Tithing is mentioned in the New Testament in Matthew, Luke, and Hebrews. The passages in Matthew 23:23 and Luke 11:42; 18:12 concern the Mosaic legislation, not the New Testament church. The historical-cultural milieu of the gospels is a people living under the Mosaic Law. The New Testament church began on the Day of Pentecost with the descent of the Holy Spirit to indwell believers. Discussions concerning the applicability of a tithe for the New Testament church are properly the concern of the apostolic era—Acts and the epistles. Therefore, the mention of tithing in Matthew and Luke are properly discussed as part of this chapter on the tithe in Mosaic times.

HISTORICAL OVERVIEW OF THE PERIOD BETWEEN JOSHUA AND MALACHI

The time between Joshua conquering the land and the prophet Malachi was approximately 1,000 years. Tithing is not mentioned between Joshua and Solomon (1405–931 BC). The fact that there is no mention of tithing in the historical narratives does not mean that people did not tithe. The silence may simply indicate the people were faithful tithers. We know that people continued to frequent the tabernacle, and later the temple, and offer sacrifices. The priests became so numerous that King David had to arrange them into groups and set dates when each group would serve in the temple. One can assume the Levites also became numerous. In the days of David and Solomon, at the least, the priests and Levites had some means of support. Either the king supported them out of civil taxes, or the people gave their tithes—whether ten percent or not—to support the religious system. Perhaps support came from both sources, with the king making up any deficiency in the tithes. After Solomon died in 931 BC the kingdom divided. The kings of the Northern Kingdom of Israel, which lasted from 931–722 BC, were uniformly bad, and the religion a syncretistic mix of YHWH and idolatry. As to the kings of the Southern Kingdom of Judah (931–605 BC), some were good and some bad. YHWH worship alternated with idolatry. This, however, does not mean that people in both the Northern and Southern Kingdoms did not tithe in some amount. Even those engaged in syncretistic worship tithed, Amos 4:4, because in their thinking they believed they were properly worshiping YHWH.

The four mentions of tithing occurring between 931 BC (after Solomon's death) and Malachi (435–400 BC) indicate the sporadic nature of tithing during this period. The first is Amos 4:4, about 650 years after Joshua and 175 years after Solomon's death. Amos mentions tithing in a negative, sarcastic manner. The people in the Northern Kingdom continued to make (at least some) tithes as part of their syncretistic religion. Amos condemned their tithes along with their religion. In the time of Hezekiah, 2 Chronicles 31, about 690 years after Joshua, and 245 years after Solomon, King Hezekiah sparked a revival of religion in the Southern Kingdom. The renewal of First Tithe was part of that revival. The revival under Hezekiah, indicates tithing, at least in Judah, was sporadic under previous kings, but not forgotten. About one hundred years later, 2 Chronicles 34–35, the temple was in disrepair. King Josiah led a revival to restore the temple and destroy the idols. A copy of the Law was found in the temple and the people had a revival and held a Passover. Tithing is not mentioned but 34:9 speaks of money the people had brought to the temple. Under the Law this would be redemption money for the first born, Leviticus 27:1–6; Numbers 18:15–16. If the people were following that part of the Law then some were probably giving tithes. The most reasonable conclusion is that tithing during the divided kingdom period was sporadic and individual, not consistent and universal. The amount tithed may not have been ten percent.

The period of the divided kingdom ended in 605 BC when Nebuchadnezzar conquered Judah and began forcibly emigrating Jews from Judah to Babylon. In 586 BC Nebuchadnezzar destroyed Jerusalem and razed the temple. Daniel and Ezekiel prophesied during this Babylonian Captivity. In 539 BC the Medo-Persians conquered Babylon, and in 538 BC Cyrus the Great issued an edict allowing captive peoples to return to their home cities, rebuild their temples, and offer prayers and sacrifices on his behalf. Some Jews returned to Jerusalem under the leadership of Zerubbabel the prince and Joshua the high priest, and began rebuilding city and temple. The temple was completed 516 BC. Nehemiah 12:47 indicates the people tithed during Zerubbabel's lifetime but stopped after his death. In 445 BC Nehemiah became governor of Judah and rebuilt the city walls. Nehemiah and Ezra sparked a revival during this time. This revival, seventy years after Zerubbabel, included a revival of First Tithe. Ten to fifteen years after Nehemiah's revival the prophet Malachi berated the people for not tithing.

While there is no information pro or con between Joshua and Solomon concerning tithing, the information between Solomon and Malachi indicates the people were not consistent in tithing. On the whole, one might say the Mosaic tithe was, as Peter states, Acts 15:10, part of the yoke of the Law "which neither our fathers nor we were able to bear."

THE TITHE FROM JOSHUA TO MALACHI

In this section I will deal with the words *'aser*, *ma'aser*, and *'asiriya*, as to their individual occurrences, and in chronological order, see the table below (all dates BC).[37]

Bible Reference	Hebrew	People and Times
1 Samuel 8:15, 17	*'asiriya*	Samuel, circa 1015
Amos 4:4, circa 755	*ma'aser*	Kings Uzziah/Amaziah, 767–750
2 Chronicles 31:5, 6, 12, 716–14	*ma'aser*	King Hezekiah, 716–687; Isaiah 742–680
Ezekiel 45:11, 14	*ma'aser*	Ezekiel, 595–568
Nehemiah 10:37, 38	*'aser*	Nehemiah, 445–433
Nehemiah 10:37, 38; 12:44; 13:5, 12	*ma'aser*	Nehemiah, 445–433
Malachi 3:8, 10	*ma'aser*	Malachi, 435–400

37. Hollingsworth, *Biblical Chronology*.

Why Christians Should Not Tithe

First Samuel 8:15, 17

The use of 'asiriya in 1 Samuel 8:15, 17 is not a reference to tithing. The people of Israel had asked Samuel to give them a king so they could have a civil government just like the Gentile nations. Samuel warns that their king will require a civil tax to support his government. Their king will take ten percent of their grain and wine to support his officers and servants, and ten percent of their sheep. This new tax will be in addition to the four tithes.

Amos 4:4

Amos 4:4 was written circa 755 BC, about 260 years after 1 Samuel and 175 years after Solomon's kingdom divided. Amos prophesied to the Northern kingdom of Israel.[38] He came as a patriot of YHWH and Israel to call the nation back to the Law and worship of the one true God. He warns of judgment on the Gentile nations and Israel. A reference to "thus says the Lord" occurs fifty-two times in 146 verses. Amos speaks about sacrifices and offerings: the burnt offerings, grain offerings, thanksgiving offerings, voluntary offerings, peace offerings, and tithes. The reference to the tithe occurs at 4:4, "Come to Bethel and transgress, at Gilgal multiply transgression; bring your sacrifices every morning, your tithes [ma'aser] every three days."

The context of this verse is the injustice and immorality of the nation, v. 1, and the punishment to come, vv. 2, 3. Verse four is sarcastic (or ironic). Bethel was, from the time of Abraham and Jacob, a place where God was worshiped, for example, Genesis 12:8; 13:3; 28:19; 31:13. When the kingdom divided following the death of Solomon, 931 BC, Jereboam I became the first king of the northern kingdom of the ten tribes of Israel (Rehoboam, Solomon's son, ruled Judah and Benjamin). Jeroboam I made an altar at Bethel, 1 Kings 12, to compete with the temple in Jerusalem. With this alternate place of worship he hoped to keep the people in his kingdom from returning to Jerusalem to make their sacrifices and offerings. He made two golden calves and Israel (ten of the twelve tribes), combined idolatry with the worship of YHWH. Gilgal was no less famous. There Joshua had set twelve stones as a memorial of the nation's entry into the promised land. The people made Saul king at Gilgal, 1 Samuel 11:15. Bethel and Gilgal are mentioned again at Amos 5:5, where the word of the

---

38. Smith and Page, *Amos, Obadiah, Jonah*, 23.

The Tithe in Mosaic Times

Lord is "seek me and live," but do not seek for me at Bethel or Gilgal. In this context Amos (YHWH through Amos, see 4:5) says that their worship at Bethel and Gilgal is a sin (because it is idolatry). The people are following the Law concerning sacrifices and offerings, vv. 4, 5. However, all their efforts were a transgression against the Lord because their worship was syncretistic: a combination of YHWH and idol worship. In this context YHWH says "bring ... your tithes after three days." Their use of the Law was according to what they thought was right, but their worship, sacrifices, offerings, and tithes were not acceptable.

The word *ma'aser* is being used properly, that is, it refers to the tithes. The passage may be referring to either the Festival Tithe or the Poor Tithe; possibly both.[39] In v. 1, Amos writes, "[you] oppress the poor ... crush the needy" and v. 5, "proclaim and announce the freewill offerings." Stuart suggests, "typical pilgrimages of the day may have lasted three days. Sacrifices ... were made on the first morning after arrival and tithes given on the third. Amos exaggerates the practice to 'every day' and 'every third day' as if the Israelites were doing nothing but making pilgrimages. Even such intense worship was odious to Yahweh. In the context, the pronoun 'your' with 'worship' and 'tithes' suggests that they were not really acceptable to Yahweh."[40] Tithing was one part of worshiping YHWH. If their worship was unacceptable, because syncretistic, then everything associated with that worship, including their tithes, was unacceptable.

Second Chronicles 31:5, 6, 12

When Hezekiah became King of Judah (the southern kingdom) in 716 BC the nation had for a long time been engaging in the syncretistic worship of YHWH and idols. Hezekiah immediately cleansed the temple and restored the temple worship. He restored the Levites and priests to their positions, and set the example for Israel, 2 Chronicles 31:3, by giving "a portion of his possessions for the burnt offerings: for the morning and evening burnt offerings, the burnt offerings for the Sabbaths and the New Moons and the set festivals, as it is written in the Law of the Lord." Hezekiah commanded the people who dwelt in Jerusalem to contribute

---

39. Compare Smith and Page, *Amos, Obadiah, Jonah*, 88.
40. Stuart, *Hosea-Jonah*, 338. Compare Cripps, *Amos*, 170. Concerning "tithes every three days," Cripps says "outside the verse itself there is no evidence for it [sacrifice on the first day after arrival at the sanctuary and tithes on the third day]."

support for the priests and Levites. In response, people throughout the kingdom, not just in Jerusalem, voluntarily responded to his call.

> Second Chronicles 31:5–7, "Israel brought in abundance the firstfruits of grain and wine, oil and honey, and of all the produce of the field; and they brought in abundantly the tithe [*ma'aser*] of everything. And the children of Israel and Judah, who dwelt in the cities of Judah, brought the tithe [*ma'aser*] of oxen and sheep; also the tithe [*ma'aser*] of holy things which were consecrated to the Lord their God they laid in heaps. In the third month they began laying them in heaps, and they finished in the seventh month."

The problem became what to do with the heaps of grain, fruit, and nuts. Hezekiah, v. 11, commanded the priests to prepare rooms in the house of the Lord to store[41] the heaps of "offerings, the tithes, and the dedicated things." So, v. 12, the priests appointed certain men to prepare the rooms and "then they faithfully brought in the offerings, the tithes [*ma'aser*], and the dedicated things" into those rooms for storage.

The tithe in this passage is First Tithe. In the revival under Hezekiah the people were concerned to fully obey the Law. They cleansed the temple, restored the worship, celebrated the Passover-Festival of Unleavened Bread (chapter 30), which had not been done in the prescribed manner for a long time, 30:5, and restored the offerings of firstfruits, dedicated things, and First Tithe. Now, they celebrated Passover in the second month, not the first month as the Law required, because a sufficient number of priests had not sanctified themselves, 30:3, to celebrate Passover-Unleavened Bread in the first month. After they had celebrated Passover-Unleavened Bread in the second month, Hezekiah commanded the people to bring in the "firstfruits of grain and wine, oil and honey, and of all the produce of the field." In response, the people "brought in abundantly the tithe of everything, between the third and seventh months." The reason I have labored over the timing is to establish that these tithes were given according to the harvest cycles, just as I suggested in an earlier discussion (When was the Agricultural Product Tithed?). The third month was May-June, when the wheat, oats, peas, lentils, and vetch harvest began. The seventh month was September-October when grapes, figs, pomegranates, and olives were harvested. In between, chickpeas, sesame, flax, and millet were harvested. Hezekiah, 30:4, "commanded the people who dwelt in

---

41. These rooms are the "storehouse" in Nehemiah 10:38 and Malachi 3:10.

Jerusalem to contribute," and, v. 5, the "children of Israel and Judah, who dwelt in the cities of Judah, brought the tithe." The revival that had begun in Jerusalem spread throughout the kingdom of Judah, and all the people responded with their tithes and offerings, just as the Law commanded.

Ezekiel 45:11, 14

The Southern Kingdom of Judah was captive to Babylon from 605 BC until the first return under Zerubbabel in 538 BC. The biblical histories (2 Kings 25; 2 Chronicles 36) do not address the remnant remaining in Israel during the Babylonian Captivity. They may have been tithing before the temple was razed in 586 BC, but after that event there was no place for their priests to minister, and therefore they had no religious system to support. A reasonable assumption is that tithing (except, perhaps, Poor Tithe) ceased after the temple was razed. The historical records of the Captivity, Daniel (605–530 BC) and Ezekiel (595–568 BC), say nothing about tithing by the captives during their captivity. Indeed, to whom would they give the tithe? They were captives in a foreign land (and the remnant in Israel under foreign rule), their temple had been destroyed, the priests and Levites continued as a people group but had no religious duties and no place to perform those duties. In their captivity the Levites and priests would have to earn their living by farming, ranching, or various occupations in the cities. The festivals, which must be celebrated in Jerusalem, were not celebrated. The people resided in Babylonian (and later, Persian) cities as expatriates, so they had no "gates" at which to systematically give a tithe to the poor (individual giving probably occurred). The tithe was "of the land," Leviticus 27:30, meaning the tithe came from the crops grown and animals raised on the land of Israel. As being outside the land there was no place where they might grow or raise a tithe, no religious service for which they might give their tithes, no Jewish city gates to store Poor Tithe, and there was no Jerusalem (or Levitical cities) to which they might send a tithe. A tithe could be grown and given only in the land of Israel. Whatever giving might have occurred in their exile was on an individual basis, and was not a tithe according to the Law.

Ezekiel prophesied just prior to the destruction of Jerusalem and then continued subsequent to that destruction as one of the Babylonian exiles. The relevant passages are:

Ezekiel 45:11, "The ephah and the bath shall be of the same measure, so that the bath contains one-tenth [*ma'aser*] of a homer, and the ephah one-tenth [*ma'aser*] of a homer; their measure shall be according to the homer."

Ezekiel 45:14, "The ordinance concerning oil, the bath of oil, is one-tenth [*ma'aser*] of a bath from a kor. A kor is a homer or ten baths, for ten baths are a homer."

The word *ma'aser* is being used in its root meaning of a tenth. The bath, homer, ephah, and kor were units of volume measurement. A kor and homer were the same volume; the ephah and bath were one-tenth the volume of the kor and homer. The passage refers to a just measurement. It does not refer to tithing.

Nehemiah 10:37, 38; 12:44

Many Jews (49,937 in the first return, Ezra 2:64–65) returned to Jerusalem after the Medo-Persians had conquered the Babylonians. The first return took place in 538 BC, described in Ezra 1–6, under the leadership of Zerubbabel the prince and Joshua the high priest.[42] The temple was rebuilt by 516 BC, with fervent exhortations from the prophets Haggai (520–505 BC) and Zechariah (520–490 BC). In 458 BC Ezra the scribe led another return, described in Ezra 7–10. The historical records of the two returns (538–516, 458–445) in the book of Ezra say nothing about tithing. The book of Esther, which takes place between Ezra chapters six and seven (486–464), has nothing to say about tithing by those Jews who chose to live outside the land of Israel after the return.[43] Nehemiah 12:47 says tithing had resumed under Zerubbabel after the temple was rebuilt: "in the days of Zerubbabel . . . all Israel gave the portions for the singers and the gatekeepers, a portion for each day. They also consecrated [the portions] for the Levites, and the Levites consecrated [the portions] for the children of Aaron." The fact that tithing had to be revived seventy years later by

---

42. That there was a high priest after the exile does not mean the priests functioned sacerdotally during the exile, but that the family of Aaron maintained its genealogical separation during the exile. The same can probably be said for all the tribe of Levi. The author of Esther knew the ancestry of Esther and Mordecai, Esther 2:5, implying the Jews continued to maintain genealogical records during their exile.

43. The events of Ezra 1–6 take place 538–516 BC. The events of Esther (Esther made Queen 478 BC) take place 486–464 BC. The events of Ezra 7–10 take place 458–445 BC. The events of Nehemiah take place 445–433 BC.

The Tithe in Mosaic Times

Ezra and Nehemiah interprets "the days of Zerubbabel": the people had stopped tithing shortly after Zerubbabel had died.

In 445 BC Nehemiah came to Jerusalem as governor of Judah and rebuilt the city walls. After the wall around Jerusalem had been rebuilt, Nehemiah gathered the people in Judah to Jerusalem, and Ezra and his fellow scribes read the Law aloud to the people, Nehemiah 8. On hearing the Law the people made a covenant to do what the Law required. As part of that covenant the people "made ordinances for ourselves," 10:32, to give everything that was needed to run the temple and religious services according to the Law. Part of those ordinances required the people,

> Nehemiah 10:37–38, "to bring the tithes [ma'aser] of our land to the Levites, for the Levites should receive the tithes ['aser] in all our farming communities. And the priest, the descendant of Aaron, shall be with the Levites when the Levites receive tithes ['aser]; and the Levites shall bring up a tenth [ma'aser] of the tithes [ma'aser] to the house of our God, to the rooms of the storehouse."

The people agreed that the Levites should receive the tenth, 'aser, "in all our farming communities,"[44] and that the priests should receive a tithe [ma'aser] of the tithes [ma'aser]. The Levites were to bring the tithe [ma'aser] of the tithes [ma'aser] to the temple "to the rooms of the storehouse." The "rooms of the storehouse" (rebuilt by Zerubbabel) were those Hezekiah had commanded be used to store First Tithe. Here, in Nehemiah, we see that the Levites collected First Tithe "in all our farming communities," from the farmer and then brought the priest's portion, the Levites' tithe [ma'aser] of the tithes [ma'aser], to the temple for storage. The ordinances the people set for themselves, some 1055 years after the Law was given,[45] show that after they had read the Law, Nehemiah 8:1–18, they interpreted Leviticus 27:30–33 and Numbers 18:21–30 just as I have explained these passages in previous discussions.

Nehemiah 12:44, 47 appear to refer to the same period of time as 10:37–38, but give more detail concerning the tithes. According to 12:44 both First and Levites' tithes were brought to Jerusalem and stored in the temple. "And at the same time some [Levites, priests] were appointed over

---

44. The Levites received the tithes at the farming communities because after the Babylonian Captivity they no longer had their own cities.

45. Modern critics believe the tithing regulations were created after the exile to support a new priesthood. There is no historical or textual reason for denying these regulations were given to Israel through Moses.

the rooms of the storehouse for the offerings, the firstfruits, and the tithes [*ma'aser*], to gather into them from the fields of the cities the portions specified by the Law for the priests and Levites; for Judah rejoiced over the priests and Levites who ministered."

The words for tithe do not appear in 12:47, but the subject is equitable distribution of First and Levites' tithes, "in the days of Nehemiah all Israel gave the portions for the singers and the gatekeepers, a portion for each day. They also consecrated [the portions] for the Levites, and the Levites consecrated [the portions] for the children of Aaron."

The tithe was not given during the captivity in Babylon, and was not resumed until Zerubbabel had rebuilt the temple. Tithing stopped sometime after Zerubbabel's death. In the revival of religion under Nehemiah and Ezra the tithe was begun anew according to the instructions in the Mosaic Law.

Nehemiah 13:5, 12

During his tenure as governor Nehemiah made several trips between Shushan and Jerusalem, returning each time to resolve various problems. The first of these verses speaks of one such problem. Nehemiah 13:5, "And he [Eliashib the priest] had prepared for him [Tobiah] a large room, where previously they had stored the grain offerings, the frankincense, the articles, the tithes of grain, the new wine and oil, which were commanded to be given to the Levites and singers and gatekeepers, and the offerings for the priests."

A little background is required. Nehemiah had originally gone to Jerusalem in the twentieth year of King Artaxerxes. In the thirty-second year of the king Nehemiah returned to Shushan. After "certain days" Nehemiah asked permission from the king to return to Jerusalem. That he asked permission supposes his term as governor of Judah had expired and he had not expected to return. This in part accounts for the actions of Eliashib. He had not expected Nehemiah to return. Eliashib the priest (not high priest, Nehemiah 3; the high priest would not be in charge of a storeroom) took one of the store rooms used for the tithes, cleaned it out, and gave it to Tobiah for his use as an office within the temple. This Tobiah was a Gentile who had opposed the rebuilding of the wall, Nehemiah 2:10, 19, 4:3, 7; 6:1, 12, 14. Tobiah, however, was connected by marriage to the Judean nobles, 6:17–19. Eliashib was "allied with Tobiah," 13:4, probably through marriage. By giving Tobiah, a Gentile, office space in the temple, Eliashib had given him a prominent place from which to affect Jewish polity. The reduced storage affected the distribution of the tithes to the Levites and priests, v. 10. When Tobiah was removed and the storage was restored, the people brought their tithes to the temple, Nehemiah 13:12, "Then all Judah brought the tithe [ma'aser] of the grain and the new wine and the oil to the storehouse."

Malachi 3:8, 10

The passage (3:8–10) reads:

> Malachi 3:8-10, "Will a man rob God? Yet you have robbed Me! But you say, 'In what way have we robbed You?' 'In tithes [ma'aser] and offerings. You are cursed with a curse, for you have robbed Me, even this whole nation. Bring all the tithes [ma'aser] into the storehouse, that there may be food in My house, and try Me now in this,' says the Lord of hosts, 'If I will not open for you the windows of heaven and pour out for you such blessing that there will not be room enough to receive it.'"

One is tempted to say that this is the most famous New Testament passage on tithing—except these are Old Testament verses addressing a people living under the Law of Moses. YHWH, speaking through Malachi (435–400 BC), accuses the nation of robbing God by not giving tithes and offerings. How can this people be fairly and accurately accused of robbing God? YHWH is the owner of the land he gave to Israel, Leviticus 23:23. The Israelites are tenants on YHWH's land. Therefore Israel owes YHWH a tithe, Leviticus 27:30-33, "all the tithe of the land . . . is YHWH's." "Concerning the tithe of the herd or flock . . . shall be holy to YHWH." When the people of Israel did not tithe, then they retained for their own use something that belonged to God. This truth is reiterated in Numbers 18:21, "behold I, YHWH, have given the children of Levi all the tithes in Israel," and v. 28, "you [Levites] shall also offer a heave offering to the Lord from all your tithes . . . and you shall give the Lord's heave offering from it to Aaron." YHWH speaks of himself as the One to whom the land of Israel belonged, and the One who had given Levi all the tithes in Israel. Israel owed the owner of the land, YHWH, a tithe from the land. The people also owed YHWH firstfruits from the fields and other similar offerings. These were the sacrifices and offerings presented at the altar of sacrifice, of which the priests had a share for personal use. More than the tithe is at issue. Just as the phrase "sacrifices and offerings" is a metonym for the entire system of worship, so the phrase "tithes and offerings" is a metonym for the all the offerings the people gave to YHWH through the priests.

The people were withholding their tithes and offerings because the system of worship was being mismanaged by the priests (3:1–3). God said to withhold the tithe was wrong. The tithes and other offerings were owed to YHWH, both as belonging to him and as a religious offering to him; therefore obedience was required. We saw this principle in Joseph's tax (Genesis 47:24), which supported both government and false religious system, but which the Israelites were required to pay. Those paying the tax were blessed for obedience; those receiving the tax were responsible to use it properly. The same was true for First Tithe and Poor Tithe. All of First Tithe had been given to the Levites and priests by YHWH. The farmer fulfilled his responsibility toward YHWH when he gave First Tithe to the Levites. The Levites' were the one's responsible to use First Tithe properly, that is, to make their tithe to the priests. The city elders were responsible to see that Poor Tithe went to the poor. The disobedience of someone else is never a reason for personal disobedience. The tithe was the Lord's, and Israel needed to give the tithe as instructed.

The tithe in view in this passage is First Tithe. The First Tithe was not being made to the Levites, therefore the nation, as a whole, except for the Levites and the priests, were "robbing" God (the Levites and priests were guilty of other sins). Given the history of the nation, and how shortly in time this statement occurs after the reforms under Ezra and Nehemiah (about 10–15 years), the failure of the people to tithe is all the more amazing. Part of the problem may be the fault of the priests, for example, 1:6–9; 2:1–9; 3:1–3. Yet, despite the failure of the priesthood, the people remained obligated to be personally faithful to God's commands—not merely the tithe, but also in matters of justice, morality, and worship, 3:5. Their failure to tithe was one of many complaints YHWH had against his people. Simply giving the First Tithe would not resolve all the problems. The promise to "open for you the windows of heaven, and pour out for you [so much] blessing that there will be no room to receive it," is given as indicative of all the blessings the nation will receive if it returns to true worship of the one true God, as reflected in their obedience to the whole Law.

The Tithe in Mosaic Times

The believer was to bring his tithe, "that there may be food in my house." The reference to food, v. 10, is literal. Food, not money, was the substance of the tithe. The reference in v. 10 to "there will not be room enough to receive it," refers secondarily to blessing the tither, but primarily to filling the "storehouse" that was "in my house." As noted earlier, the "storehouse" was the rooms in the temple complex used to store First Tithe and Levites' Tithe. The storehouse was Hezekiah's solution to five months of tithes gathered in heaps on the floor of the temple complex. Hezekiah's storehouse was Nehemiah's solution—an historical solution—to collect the abundant tithes and other offerings the people brought to the rebuilt temple and renewed worship. Malachi's exhortations are set in the context of Nehemiah's recent reforms. Under Nehemiah's reforms, the normal course of giving to support the religious system required the tithes to be brought to the temple complex for storage and later disbursement. YHWH, through Malachi, exhorts the people of Israel to resume tithing and bring their tithes into the storerooms in the temple complex.[46]

The "storehouse" concept has been so misused in this New Testament age, that it is necessary to say the New Testament temple is the believer, not a building, and there is no such thing in the apostolic writings as a New Testament church building, nor a storehouse for tithes and offerings. The people are the church; the individual believer is the storehouse from which the church's ministries are supplied, 1 Corinthians 16:2; 2 Corinthians 9:7. Should there be a building for the church to use, it is not as a storehouse but as a house of worship, evangelism, and discipleship. The tithe in Malachi must be interpreted by Leviticus 27, Numbers 18, and Deuteronomy 12, 14, and 26, and applied to a people with 1100 years of history living under the Mosaic Law.

THE TITHE FROM MALACHI TO JESUS

Information on tithing in these times is limited to various books, commentaries and histories written (sometimes centuries) after the fact. The main source materials are the apocryphal books from the second century BC; the Mishnah, which was compiled between 200 BC–AD 200; comments

---

46. Since Malachi began his ministry in 435 BC, these exhortations might be in the context of the problems caused by Eliashib and Tobiah, Nehemiah 13:4–12, which took place about 433 BC.

by the Jewish philosopher Philo; and comments by the Jewish historian Josephus.

The apocryphal book of Jubilees was written about 135–105 BC. In chapter 32 its author resolves the issue of Jacob's tithe, Genesis 28, 35, by anachronistically speaking of it in terms of the Festival Tithe. The apocryphal book of Tobit, written about the same time as Jubilees, states at 1:6–8,

> Tobit 1:6–8, "But I went alone many a time to Jerusalem for the festivals, as the Scripture commands all Israel in an everlasting decree, taking with me the first fruits and the tenth parts of my crops and my first shearings [see Deuteronomy 18:4] , and I would give them to the priests, the sons of Aaron, at the altar. A tenth part of all my produce I would give to the sons of Levi, who officiated at Jerusalem, and another tenth I would sell, and go spend the proceeds in Jerusalem each year, and the third year I would give to those to whom it was fitting to give it, as Deborah my grandmother had instructed me—for I was left an orphan by my father."[47]

The writer of Tobit indicates that in the second century BC devout Jews were giving First, Festival, and Poor Tithes.

The Mishnah, in tractates *Demi*, *Maaseroth*, and *Maaser Shemi*, addresses in tedious detail the traditions the rabbis developed concerning tithing. The Pharisees were responsible for many of these regulations, and in their zeal to protect the Law they made the tithe a burden. A tithe, no matter how small was extracted from everyone. God's simple instructions were expanded to ridiculous and minute details. The tractate *Demi* describes exceptions to tithes—except that there are exceptions to the exceptions. For example, all sycamore figs are exempt excepting those that ripen on the tree until they break open; what was given to one's wife or mother-in-law for cooking must be tithed before given to her and when returned from her. The tractate *Maaseroth* describes what must be tithed in tediously excruciating detail. For example, a detailed description of when various produce becomes liable to tithes; produce eaten outside a house or business was not liable to tithes, but produce brought into a house or business was liable to tithes; a laborer harvesting fruit was not liable for a tithe on the fruit he might eat, but a son harvesting fruit was liable for the fruit he might eat; replanted seedlings (already fit for food) if uprooted and replanted were not liable to tithes, but if sold at market they

---

47. *Apocrypha*, 109.

The Tithe in Mosaic Times

were liable to tithes; what was found in an ant-hole near a heap of corn was liable to tithes. The tractate *Maaser Shemi* describes Festival Tithe.

Philo, 20 BC–AD 50, a Jew who lived in Alexandria, Egypt, speaks of the First Tithe and Levites' Tithe (not, of course, using those terms). He wrote that the tithes were "the source of revenue of no insignificance to the priests" bidding them to take "the first fruits of every revenues of the nation, namely, the firstfruits of the corn, and wine, and oil, and even the produce of all the cattle, or the flocks of sheep, and herds of oxen, and flocks of goats, and all other animals of all kinds."[48] Josephus, the Jewish historian who lived AD 37 to circa AD 100, wrote in *Antiquities*, 4.8.22, "besides those two tithes, which I have already said you are to pay every year, the one for the Levites [First tithe], the other for the festivals [Festival Tithe], you are to bring every third year a third [Poor] tithe to be distributed to those that want." Schurer, 1884–1910, states "in post-biblical times [he means between Malachi and Jesus] the entire passage [Leviticus 27:30–33] was understood as referring to the tithe prescribed by Deuteronomy."[49] These various works indicate the tithes, in one form or another, continued during the intertestamental period.

By the time of Jesus the Jews known as Pharisees had made a revival of tithing according to their strict traditions. In the time between Malachi and Jesus Israel had experienced severe repression and persecution under a number of Gentile rulers. The religious among the nation developed into several sects as a result of these trials. We know these sects as Sadducees, Pharisees, and Essenes. The Pharisees believed Israel's failure to follow the Law was the main cause of the nation's troubles. Members of this sect began an intense study of the Law, analyzing it to the most minute jot and tittle. They developed a philosophy designed to protect the Law from being broken. The main thrust of that philosophy was that the Pharisees would develop laws and traditions more stringent than the Mosaic Law which, if scrupulously followed, would protect the Mosaic Law from being broken. In effect, they decided to build a fence around the Law with their own interpretations and traditions. If no one crossed the fence, then the Mosaic Law would never be broken, and the nation would be saved from future persecution and destruction. Over time these traditions came to be viewed as just as important and binding as the Law. In practice many

48. Philo, *Works, The Special Laws 1*, sections 141, 148.
49. Schurer, *History*, 2:255.

of the traditions broke the Law, as Jesus illustrates, for example, Matthew 15:1–6. The Pharisees' rules about tithing, seen in their boast concerning a tithe of mint, anise, and cummin, Matthew 23:23, was the product of that philosophy. The Gospels give no information concerning tithing by the rest of the population.

THE TITHE IN THE GOSPELS

The events in the Gospels take place under the Old Testament Mosaic economy. Jesus was a son of the Law who faithfully obeyed the Mosaic Covenant. The New Testament church age began under a New Covenant (Hebrews 8:6–13; 10:16–18) after Jesus' resurrection and ascension. Therefore, any mention of tithing in the Gospels falls under the instructions and commandments given in the Mosaic Law. The Greek word *apodekatoo*, "to tithe from," occurs at Matthew 23:23; Luke 11:42; Luke 18:12.

> Matthew 23:23, "Woe to you, scribes and Pharisees, hypocrites! For you pay tithe of mint and anise and cummin, and have neglected the weightier matters of the law: justice and mercy and faith. These you ought to have done, without leaving the others undone."

> Luke 11:42, "But woe to you Pharisees! For you tithe mint and rue and all manner of herbs, and pass by justice and the love of God. These you ought to have done, without leaving the others undone."

> Luke 18:12, "I fast twice a week; I give tithes of all that I possess."

The passages in Matthew 23:23 and Luke 11:42 are their respective writer's perspective on the same event. Luke 18:12 occurs in the parable of the self-righteous Pharisee. These verses are hardly a call for New Testament believers to tithe. They concern the most legalistic sect of Judaism in an activity where they believed they excelled in righteousness over other Jews. Jesus is not commending them.

In the Matthew 23:23 and Luke 11:42 passages Jesus is saying that the Pharisees will take great care to tithe on the spices they use, so that they meet the most exacting requirements of their tradition, but cannot be bothered to take an interest in justice, mercy, and faith, which are the heart of the Law. The biblical rules concerning tithing did not require the Pharisees, or anyone else, to tithe on the spices they bought at market or used in their cooking. They had substituted their traditions on tithing for more serious matters. They allowed themselves to sin the greater sins while avoiding the smallest sins. The smaller sins are the most obvious sins, the most public and visible sins. The greater sins are matters such as injustice, cruelty, inequity, and no-faith; indifference toward the greater sins can be hidden under the guise of religious affectation. When Jesus said, "These you ought to have done, without leaving the others undone," he was not commending their tithing; he was saying that obedience to the whole Law is required. Matthew 23:24 makes this very plain. Verse 24, to strain out a gnat but swallow a camel, was a proverbial-type saying. The gnat was the smallest unclean animal, Leviticus 11:41, and the camel the largest unclean animal, Leviticus 11:4. Used figuratively, the saying meant the Pharisees were careful to follow the smallest and most inconsequential aspects of the Law as altered by their traditions, but were guilty of ignoring, thus breaking, the most consequential and gravest aspects of the Law. A principle that may be drawn from these passages is that one righteous work does not relieve the believer from the obligation to be righteous in all his works. Put another way, giving is not a substitute for the other obligations of Christianity. The parable in Luke 18:10–14 follows the same view. The Pharisee counted his faithfulness in tithing as one of the works that he supposed made him righteous with God. The tax collector confessed his sin and prayed for salvation. The Pharisee congratulated himself that his moral life and good works made him righteous enough for God. Jesus says a moral life and good works are no substitute for a salvific relationship with God. Neither of these passages teaches the New Testament believer to tithe. They do teach that appropriate religious giving is one small part of the larger Christian life.

SUMMARY OF THE TITHE IN OLD TESTAMENT TIMES

The act of giving to support religion is part of man's history. Throughout history the act of religious giving has been called a tithe. The amount given varied until the Mosaic Law. The Israelites, like the rest of the world at that time, were spiritually immature in their understanding of YHWH and his worship. YHWH established a specific form of worship for Israel. That form of worship gave them little room for innovation, as it prescribed the time, manner, place, and result of its required sacrifices and offerings. As to the tithe, it conformed to the people's historical and religious expectations. God is to be supported by religious giving; religious giving is given to the priests who mediate God to the people. God prescribed exactly what would be given as a tithe. He prescribed the exact amount to be given. He prescribed the persons who would give the tithes and the persons who would receive the tithes. In the case of the Festival and Poor Tithes he prescribed where the tithe would be given and what it would be used for. The four tithes supported both groups of God's people: the full time religious professional and the "secular" worshiper. For this one people, in their particular historical economy, according to their peculiar form of worship, God prescribed everything, including how his ministers would be supported by the people to whom they ministered.

4

The Tithe in Apostolic Times

THE TITLE OF THIS chapter is something of a misnomer, since there is no tithe prescribed by the apostles for the New Testament church age. The word *apodekatoo*, "to tithe from," occurs once in the apostolic writings, Hebrews 7:5. The word *dekate*, "a tenth part," occurs at Hebrews 7:2, 4, 8, 9. The word *dekatoo*, "to give or take a tenth," occurs at Hebrews 7:6, 9. None of these uses are an instruction to the New Testament church to make a tithe. Since Acts and the epistles do not mention tithing, the plan of this chapter is to examine the historical instances where the apostles and other New Testament authors had an opportunity to teach giving by tithing. From their writings, I will develop twenty-one principles that guide New Testament giving.

THE BOOK OF ACTS

The book of Acts affords many opportunities to teach tithing, but the concept and practice are missing from the book. Each passage by itself is not a conclusive argument against a New Testament tithe. Taken as a whole they are a powerful testimony that the early church did not practice the Mosaic tithe, or some type of giving based on tithing, to support the New Testament church. As Jews who believed in the Jewish Messiah, one might have expected them have diverted some or all of their tithes to support the newly formed church. That they did not is a very convincing argument against a New Testament tithe.

Why Christians Should Not Tithe

Acts 4:32–35

The verses are:

> Acts 4:32–35, "Now the multitude of those who believed were of one heart and one soul; neither did anyone say that any of the things he possessed was his own, but they had all things in common. And with great power the apostles gave witness to the resurrection of the Lord Jesus. And great grace was upon them all. Nor was there anyone among them who lacked; for all who were possessors of lands or houses sold them, and brought the proceeds of the things that were sold, and laid them at the apostles' feet; and they distributed to each as anyone had need."

For the first seven to ten years of its existence (from Pentecost, May, AD 33 to circa AD 40–43), the New Testament church was exclusively Hebrew people converted from Judaism to Christianity.[1] Acts 5:20 reveals the source of the earliest converts to Christianity, "Go, stand in the temple and speak to the people all the words of this life." The early Hebrew Christians considered themselves as the next step in Judaism: God's people with faith in Jesus the Messiah. They saw little or no conflict between their faith in Jesus and the Mosaic Law, and would have been offended if someone had suggested they could stop living according to the Mosaic regulations. Even as late as AD 58 Paul is told by James (half-brother of the Lord and leader of the Jerusalem church), "how many myriads[2] of Jews there are that have believed, and they are all zealous for the Law," Acts 21:20. Under these circumstances one might have expected them to have diverted their tithes from the temple to the newly born church, but they continued to tithe to the temple.

The followers of Jesus the Christ suffered disapproval and persecution. Their basic needs were food and shelter. The Mosaic tithe was designed to meet the first, so that money could be spent on the second. Here was an opportunity for the Holy Spirit to divert the tithe to the New Testament church. Perhaps few of these new Christians were farmers, although under rabbinical tradition every Jew tithed something. Yet, the tithe was not the way in which the early church met its needs. Instead they possessed all things in common, sold lands and houses, and brought the

---

1. Cornelius the Gentile, Acts 10, was saved between AD 40–43.

2. A *myriad* was the highest number in the ancient world, and means 10,000. "Myriads of Jews who have believed," means many ten thousands of Jews who have believed.

money from the sale to the apostles for distribution to "anyone" in need. A gift of money is not a tithe, but if this was a use of Poor Tithe, or from principles based on that tithe, then Luke and the Holy Spirit missed their opportunity to say so. The Spirit could have led the apostles to require a percentage of the sales, using the Old Testament example as a starting principle for New Testament giving. However, here was something completely new. The believers followed a new principle: total dedication of self and possessions to the cause of the gospel. Communal possessions in those early days did not establish a norm for later Christianity, as the epistles make clear. Nor should one assume that those who sold lands and houses sold the very house they were living in or the lands that provided them an income. A little common sense is required. The meaning, in modern terms, is that they sold their real estate investment properties. If one sold his primary home, then he would have no place to live, and would have become one of the poor he was trying to help. Nor would he have been able to offer living quarters to those Jews who lived in Gentile lands, had come to Jerusalem for the festivals, Acts 2:8–11, were converted to Christianity, and remained in Jerusalem after their conversion. Christianity does not require one to give everything, but it does require that everything should be available for use by the Lord. That is the principle the early Christians followed. In following that principle, they gave according to what they had to support the needs of their church.

Acts 5:1–4

The verses are:

> Acts 5:1–4, "But a certain man named Ananias, with Sapphira his wife, sold a possession. And he kept back part of the proceeds, his wife also being aware of it, and brought a certain part and laid it at the apostles' feet. But Peter said, 'Ananias, why has Satan filled your heart to lie to the Holy Spirit and keep back part of the price of the land for yourself? While it remained, was it not your own? And after it was sold, was it not in your own control? Why have you conceived this thing in your heart? You have not lied to men but to God.'"

The deception perpetrated by Ananias and Sapphira was an opportunity for Peter and the Holy Spirit to put a tithe-like face on Christian giving. These two had sold a possession. They received a certain amount of money from the sale and decided to give part of their proceeds to the church. As 4:32–35 indicate there was no compulsion to give; neither were believers compelled to give all. What one gave was decided by the individual, not the church. However, Ananias and Sapphira pretended as though the part they gave was the whole. Their sin was not in keeping part of the whole; their sin was pretending the part they gave was the whole amount they received from the sale of their land.[3]

Peter was made aware of their sin by the Holy Spirit, directly or through some means not stated. The question relevant to a discussion of tithing is, why didn't Peter and the Holy Spirit take advantage of the opportunity to tell Christians what portion of the whole should have been given? Believers were selling lands and houses to get money to support the poor of the church. Many had lost jobs because they believed in Jesus as Messiah; many who lived in Gentile lands had remained in Jerusalem following their conversion (Acts 2:9–11). Why not follow the principles of tithing from the Law and use a tithe of the money to support these poor? The apostles themselves needed support as they dedicated themselves to study the Word of God. Why not consider the apostles priests of the church and give a First Tithe from the sale of lands and houses to support these new priests?

Here was the time and place for Peter to say, "When you sell a possession and want to give the proceeds to the church, you may give all of those proceeds if you choose, but at the least you should give a tithe. Just as Moses in the Law commanded our ancestors to give a tithe of their property to support the priests and the poor, you should tithe to support us apostles and the poor believers in Jesus the Messiah." However, Peter and the Spirit let the moment pass without instructing the people on how to give to support the church's leaders and poor, nor (more to the point of this discussion) how much to give. How much the people gave out of the proceeds of those sales was at their discretion. They weren't required to give all, or even a tithe, but they were required to be honest as to what they gave.

---

3. The word translated "kept back," v. 2, means to illegally appropriate, as in embezzlement. By pretending to give the whole, the part they kept was, in effect, embezzled from the church. The interpretation, that they dishonestly represented the part given as though it were the whole proceeds, is well supported by other commentators, for example, Alexander, *Acts*, 190; Bruce, *Acts*, 113.

The Tithe in Apostolic Times

Acts 6:1–2

The verses are:

> Acts 6:1–2, "Now in those days, when the number of the disciples was multiplying, there arose a complaint against the Hebrews by the Hellenists, because their widows were neglected in the daily distribution. Then the twelve summoned the multitude of the disciples and said, 'It is not desirable that we should leave the word of God and serve tables.'"

Here was another opportunity to establish a principle of tithing to support the church. There is no mention of giving in this passage, but there is a distribution of money. First, I should explain the "murmuring against the Hebrews by the Hellenists." The "Hebrews" were those Hebrews who lived in Israel. The "Hellenists" were those Hebrews who lived outside of Israel, descendants of many generations who were forcibly emigrated out of Israel by various Gentile persecutions and military victories, or had voluntarily left to seek their fortunes in the Gentile world. They were known as "Hellenists" because their exposure to the Greco-Roman world had influenced their interpretation of Scripture and practice of Judaism. In practical terms the word "Hellenists" identified Jews of the *diaspora*, a word meaning Jews living outside Israel. Many *diaspora* Jews returned to Jerusalem each year for the festivals. They are mentioned in Acts 2:9–11 as present at Peter's Day-of-Pentecost speech. After their conversion many remained in Jerusalem, where they had little means of local support. The money being collected in Acts 4:35 was to be used to support the poor "Hebrew" widows and the poor "Hellenist" widows. The widows in the Old Testament received a portion of Poor Tithe. The apostles had a sure guide in the Old Testament Law on how to use a tithe to support the poor. These principles could have been applied to the church's distribution of money to widows. If those principles had been followed, so that every widow received an equal portion of the money, then the Hellenists would not have had occasion to complain. Some scheme, based on tithing, could have been instituted. However, the Holy Spirit, through the apostles, decided on other means to distribute the money, and gave no guidance from tithing. At this point someone may say, We don't know how the apostles instructed the seven men. Exactly, that is the very point. Based on what the Holy Spirit has told us, the distribution was left to the discretion of the church, not regulated by a reference to Old Testament Law.

Why Christians Should Not Tithe

Acts 11:27–29

The verses are:

> Acts 11:27–29, "And in these days prophets came from Jerusalem to Antioch. Then one of them, named Agabus, stood up and showed by the Spirit that there was going to be a great famine throughout all the world, which also happened in the days of Claudius Caesar. Then the disciples, each according to his ability, determined to send relief to the brethren dwelling in Judea."

In these verses a prophecy is made concerning a "great famine throughout all the [Greco-Roman] world," which the writer notes did happen in the days of Claudius Caesar.[4] This incident reveals something about the way the church approached giving. The Christians living outside Judea, "each according to his own ability, determined to send relief to the brethren dwelling in Judea." Why didn't each disciple determine to send a tithe of his possessions to support the brethren? The Law included a tithe to relieve the suffering of the poor. Why didn't the early church give according to the Old Testament principle of giving through a tithe? The fact is, as far as this example of New Testament church giving reveals, a principle of tithing was not involved. Instead, a different principle was used. A tithe is giving regulated by law, but the church gives "each according to his own ability."

The principle of New Testament giving in this passage is: "each gives according to his own ability," Acts 11:29.

Acts 15:1–29

The applicable verses are vv. 5, 10, 19–21.

> Acts 15:5, "But some of the sect of the Pharisees who believed rose up, saying, 'It is necessary to circumcise them [the Gentile Christians], and to command them to keep the Law of Moses.'"

> Acts 15:10, "why do you test God by putting a yoke on the neck of the [Gentile] disciples which neither our fathers nor we were able to bear?"

> Acts 15:19–21, "Therefore I [James] judge that we [Hebrew Christians] should not trouble those from among the Gentiles who are turning to God, but that we write to them to abstain from

---

4. Claudius Caesar reigned AD 41–54.

things polluted by idols, from sexual immorality, from things strangled, and from blood. For Moses has had throughout many generations those who preach him in every city, being read in the synagogues every Sabbath."

The first church council was held about AD 50 to decide how to deal with Gentile Christians.[5] The issues are stated in v. 5. The Pharisees who believed [in Jesus as the Messiah] also believed Gentile Christians should be circumcised and *keep the Law of Moses* (emphasis mine). Peter's reply is to the point. The Law of Moses was a yoke neither their ancestors nor they were able to bear. Why (to summarize Peter, vv. 7–11) require the Gentile believers to keep Moses' Law when no one who had lived under that Law had achieved righteousness by being obedient to it? The council agreed. Their instructions to the Gentiles in the churches was not designed to put the yoke of the Law upon them, but simply to help them not give offense to their Hebrew Christian brethren, v. 29.

Explaining why the four things in v. 29 were singled out from the Law is beyond the scope of this discussion on tithing. However, it is appropriate to note that tithing could have been included in this letter as the means to support the churches. As James says, v. 21, some of these Gentile Christians had been proselytes to Judaism and therefore knew the Old Testament. If tithing was important to Christianity, then they already had a background in the Law that would lead them to accept tithing as the means to support their church. If the Hebrew Christians were using some scheme of giving based on tithing, then for their Gentile brethren to not follow the same scheme would have been offensive; not to mention inequitable. If the Hebrew Christians knew that tithing was the way God intended the New Testament church to be supported, then why didn't they instruct the Gentiles to tithe? That they did not argues that the Hebrew Christians were not tithing to support the church, nor giving by any principle that might have been drawn from the tithe.

---

5. Cornelius the Gentile had been saved about ten years earlier. Paul had made his first missionary journey, Acts 13–14, during AD 46–48. As the number of Gentile Christians grew, some Hebrew Christians insisted they be circumcised, Acts 15:1. A church council was convened in AD 50 to deal with this issue.

Acts 20:33–35

The verses are:

> Acts 20:33–35, "I have coveted no one's silver or gold or apparel. Yes, you yourselves know that these hands have provided for my necessities, and for those who were with me. I have shown you in every way, by laboring like this, that you must support the weak. And remember the words of the Lord Jesus, that He said, 'It is more blessed to give than to receive.'"

This word to the Ephesian elders was repeated to the Corinthians (1 Corinthians 9:15). Paul says he supported himself in order to preach the gospel. Although Paul chose to support himself, he could have mentioned that he forsook his right to be supported by a tithe. Paul had shown them through his own example how to "support the weak." Since the context is "I provided for my necessities" (through his job as a tent maker, Acts 18:2; and teaching? 19:9) then "weak" must include the "poor." The example of Poor Tithe was well known to Paul, and to the Ephesian church, who were a mixed congregation of former Hebrew Jews, former Gentile proselytes to Judaism, and former Gentile pagans. He could have mentioned the tithe as a means to support the "weak" in the church. If one's labors are to be used to support the poor, then Paul wasted an opportunity to use the Old Testament principle of the tithe to instruct these Christians on how they were to use the fruit of their labor to support the poor. Instead, Paul gave them a principle of giving that was not based on tithing: it is more blessed to give than to receive. A tithe is a legal obligation that one must give, but sharing equitably and giving willingly brings personal joy.

Acts 28:30

The verse is: Acts 28:30, "Then Paul dwelt two whole years in his own rented house, and received all who came to him." There is no need to labor on this point. Paul could have promoted tithing as a way for the churches to support him as he lived in "his own rented house." It seems unlikely Paul continued to make tents while chained to a Roman soldier. A tithe from the local church would have helped him in his economic distress. Instead he depended on voluntary giving, for example, Philippians 4:10–18.

The Tithe in Apostolic Times

THE EPISTLES

There are a few verses in Romans one might press into this discussion, such as 12:13; 13:7–8; 15:25–27. However, in 1 Corinthians 9 and 2 Corinthians 8, 9 Paul speaks directly to the issue of Christian giving.

First Corinthians 9:9–14

The "gospel" is both the good news of how sinners can be saved and instruction to the saved on Christian living. The gospel ministry is both preaching salvation to sinners and teaching believers the Word of God. First Corinthians 9:9–14 is a key passage regarding how the New Testament church is to support gospel ministers and ministries. As such, an extended discussion is warranted. The verses are:

> First Corinthians 9:9–14, "For it is written in the Law of Moses, 'You shall not muzzle an ox while it treads out the grain.' Is it oxen God is concerned about? Or does He say it altogether for our sakes? For our sakes, no doubt, this is written, that he who plows should plow in hope, and he who threshes in hope should be partaker of his hope. If we have sown spiritual things for you, is it a great thing if we reap your material things? If others are partakers of this right over you, are we not even more? Nevertheless we have not used this right, but endure all things lest we hinder the gospel of Christ. Do you not know that those who minister the holy things eat of the things of the temple, and those who serve at the altar partake of the offerings of the altar? Even so the Lord has commanded that those who preach the gospel should live from the gospel."

In certain passages in 1 Corinthians Paul defends his divine call to be an apostle. Chapter nine begins as such a passage.[6] Beginning in v. 1, Paul states he is an apostle, independent of any human control, called by Jesus Christ to be an apostle. The Corinthians' salvation as a result of his ministry was evidence of his right to be an apostle. Apparently Peter, perhaps others, 1:12, 9:5, had visited the Corinthian church in the past. These visits had generated a question as to who was an apostle, perhaps

---

6. Many commentators connect 9:15 with chapter eight and interpret 9:9–14 as part of an argument that, since Paul has denied himself in the matter of support so as not to offend the Corinthians, then those who believed in eating meat offered to idols could deny themselves that liberty for the sake of their brethren who might be offended. Such an interpretive connection is plausible, but the ideas expressed in 9:9–14 should not be ignored. Paul could (and did) deny himself support from the church, but the church does have an obligation to support those who live for the gospel, v. 14.

based on certain things said and actions taken. It would seem that those who had visited in the past had accepted support (money? food? shelter?) from the church, but Paul had chosen to support himself, 9:6, 15. Since Paul had not accepted support from the church, did he have apostolic authority? The issue is stated in vv. 3–6.

> First Corinthians 9:3–6, "My defense to those who examine me is this: Do we have no right to eat and drink? Do we have no right to take along a believing wife, as do also the other apostles, the brothers of the Lord, and Cephas? Or is it only Barnabas and I who have no right to refrain from working?"

Paul says his privilege as an apostle was the right to refrain from working and require the church to maintain him at their cost. He uses several illustrations in v. 7 to make the point.

> First Corinthians 9:7, "Who ever goes to war at his own expense? Who plants a vineyard and does not eat of its fruit? Or who tends a flock and does not drink of the milk of the flock?"

The soldier served the state and the state was responsible to support the soldier. A tenant farmer who worked the vineyard paid a portion of the fruit to the owner while retaining a portion for himself. The hired shepherd who tended a flock for the owner was free to use the milk for his own needs. These were well known customs of the culture.[7] Their meaning is that Paul, who was a soldier in the Lord's army, and was tending the Lord's vineyard, and shepherding the Lord's sheep, had the authority to claim support from the Corinthians, whose salvation was that field of battle, and who were themselves that vineyard and that flock. The gospel minister has the right to live from his labor.[8]

In vv. 8–10 Paul draws out a principle from the Mosaic Law that says the same as the previous examples from Greco-Roman culture.

> First Corinthians 9:8–10, "Do I say these things as a mere man? Or does not the law say the same also? For it is written in the law of Moses, 'You shall not muzzle an ox while it treads out the grain.' Is it oxen God is concerned about? Or does He say it altogether for our sakes? For our sakes, no doubt, this is written, that he who plows should plow in hope, and he who threshes in hope should be partaker of his hope."

---

7. See Ramsay, *Historical Commentary*, 149.
8. Hodge, *First Corinthians*, 156.

The Scripture quoted is Deuteronomy 25:4. Grain was separated from the stalks by beating the stalks, walking on the stalks, or having a large heavy animal, an oxen, walk on the stalks. The Law viewed the oxen as in partnership with the farmer, the same as the soldier employed by the state, the tenant working in another's vineyard, or the hired shepherd tending another's flock. The oxen's labor earned him a portion of the grain as his wages. God does care for the oxen, but what Paul is saying is that the Law was given for the sake of God's people.[9] Paul repeats this argument in 1 Timothy 5:18, "For the Scripture says, 'You shall not muzzle an ox while it treads out the grain,' and, 'The laborer is worthy of his wages.'" The reference to sowing and reaping, v. 10, illustrates this same principle. The one who plows does so in the hope of sharing in the harvest—indeed, a share in the harvest is his due for his labor.

Verse 11 carries the principle to the New Testament church. If Paul has sown in the Lord's fields, should he not reap from the Lord's fields? Paul is sowing spiritual things—salvation, principles for living the Christian life—but one cannot eat and drink spiritual things. Therefore, since Paul's spiritual sowing has caused a benefit to the Corinthians, is he not, as the soldier, farmer, shepherd, oxen, and sower, allowed to reap material blessings from the Corinthians? Others in spiritual authority used that right. Paul has as much or more authority to claim material benefit from the Corinthians. He chose not to, lest in the beginning of their faith journey they be hindered (as though he worked for material benefit, not for their spiritual good). However, it is the right and privilege of the gospel minister to live from his labors.

The question is, in what manner are material benefits, if and when claimed, to be collected and distributed to those with the right to receive them? What principles were to guide the New Testament church in their giving to support gospel ministers? The answer is important, because the issue goes far in time beyond the apostles, far in time beyond the Corinthian church. If Paul was going to teach tithing as the means to support gospel ministers, then this occasion was the golden opportunity. The tithe helped support the full-time workers and ministers of the Old Testament "church." The tithe was part of the support for those who ministered "the holy things," which is what gospel ministers do. If Paul was going to teach the New Testament church some model or pattern of giving

---

9. Ibid, 157.

based on Old Testament tithing, here is his opportunity. But, he does not; he very carefully states principles of giving in such a way that he cannot be misunderstood as teaching the Old Testament tithe applied to the New Testament church.

Let me repeat vv. 13–14 so we have them before us:

> First Corinthians 9:13–14, "Do you not know that those who minister the holy things eat of the things of the temple, and those who serve at the altar partake of the offerings of the altar? Even so the Lord has commanded that those who preach the gospel should live from the gospel."

Paul refers to "those who minister the holy things," and "those who serve at the altar." Opinions as to whom Paul is referring to have been variously divided. Some believe both phrases refer to the Old Testament priests; others that the first phrase refers to the Levites and the second to the priests. The third view is, "the first denotes the Levitical order as a whole (Levites and priests together), and the second, the priests only."[10] This last seems the most correct interpretation. The first phrase very generally describes all those who served in the temple, whereas the second applies to none but the priests. Thus, v. 13 may be read, "Do you not know that the tribe of Levi who minister the holy things eat of the things of the temple, and the priests who serve at the altar partake of the offerings of the altar?"

The "holy things" were the heave offerings (which included the tithe), the animal sacrifices, and other offerings, such as the peace offering and the freewill offerings. Paul narrows the focus: the priests lived from the sacrifices and offerings made at the altar. Those who served at the altar were supported by the sacrifices and offerings brought to the altar by those on whose behalf they ministered. Paul does not mention the tithe for two reasons. One, Christianity does not have a group of people who correspond to the Old Testament Levites, so the tithe to the Levites and the Levites' tithe to the priests, are not applicable. Two, the principle learned at the altar was that those who are dedicated, full time ministers live from their ministry. Paul has created a comparison to teach New Testament giving: just as those who served at the altar lived from the altar, even so those who serve the gospel should live from the gospel. The Lord has appointed that those whose life-work is to preach the gospel should

---

10. Godet, *First Corinthians*, 449.

be supported by the "proceeds" of the gospel, that is, as v. 11 says, reaping material benefits from spiritual sowing.

"The Lord has commanded that those who preach the gospel should live from the gospel" (NIV: "should receive their living from the gospel"; HCSB: "should earn their living by the gospel"; NASB95: "to get their living from the gospel"). Just as God ordained support for the religious system under the Law, even so he has ordained the means of support for the New Testament church. When Paul says, v. 14, "the Lord has commanded," he is referring to an established practice in the apostolic community, as evidenced by 9:5–6.[11] Other believers volunteer their time to the church and continue in their secular employments. But the Lord appointed certain believers to occupy the position of full time minister of the gospel (cf. Ephesians 4:11–13). Therefore, men and women dedicated to the gospel ministry,

> "renounce every secular occupation to consecrate all their time and powers to the development of the spiritual life in others [cf. Acts 6:2]; consequently the Church to which they thus consecrate their life is bound to provide for their material support . . . Such is the foundation of the institution of the Christian ministry. The object of Jesus in establishing it was not to institute a new priesthood as a new mediatorship between God and the church; but neither did Jesus wish to abandon the development of his work to the spontaneous zeal of the faithful . . . he avoided [these two choices] and confined himself to instituting a *ministry* to preach and have the cure [spiritual maintenance] of souls, the members of which live *for* the gospel, and consequently ought also to live *of* the gospel."[12]

Like the offerings given to the Old Testament priests for the altar, even so the offerings given to ministers of the gospel are holy things: Paul is "not making an argument from analogy, but represents the maintenance of the ministers at the hands of the churches as being truly an application of a principle acted upon under the Old Testament; that principle is that

---

11. When did the Lord command this practice? Paul is either referring to an unknown saying of Jesus, or principles of giving derived from Scripture. Whichever is the case, from the beginning, Acts 4:34–35, the New Testament church did not use the tithe as a means of financial support.

12. Godet, *First Corinthians*, 451 (emphasis Godet).

their maintenance is, not an earthly and secular matter, but a spiritual offering to God."[13]

Paul says of himself, Like the priests who partake of what has been sacrificed, I have a right to support from the church, but for the sake of others I do not. Paul had, in fact, received support from other churches in order to minister to the Corinthians, 2 Corinthians 8:1; 11:8. The point should be plain: the Christian church and its ministers of the gospel are not supported by a tithe, but by the principle that underlay the tithe and gave portions of the sacrifices to the priests: offerings are given to God to support his ministers. In the church, material support for ministers and ministries comes from the place where the work is done, which is to say, from those who benefit from the gospel. Christ did not establish a new priesthood, nor an order of workers in some new temple; these things are contrary to Christianity. The New Testament church did not and does not have a religious order like the Levites. Nor does the New Testament church have an order of priests mediating God to the people. Every New Testament believer is a priest with direct access to God through Jesus Christ. The Lord calls some believers to minister spiritual things to others. The Old Testament priests lived from the altar where they ministered, receiving grain and meat from those to whom they ministered spiritual things. Even so, the Lord has ordained that those whom he calls to live *for* the gospel are to live *from* the gospel, v. 14, reaping material things from those to whom they minister spiritual things. Such support is not a tithe but an offering to God with a sweet fragrance. The principles of New Testament giving in this passage are:

- The laborer is worthy of his wages, 1 Corinthians 9:7–9 (cf. 1 Timothy 5:18)
- Those who reap support those who sow, 1 Corinthians 9:10
- Those who sow spiritual things should reap material things, 1 Corinthians 9:11
- Give regularly, 1 Corinthians 9:13 (there were daily, weekly, and monthly sacrifices and offerings in the Old Testament economy)
- Those who live for the gospel should live from the gospel, 1 Corinthians 9:14

---

13. Edwards, *First Corinthians*, 232–33.

The Tithe in Apostolic Times

First Corinthians 16:1–3

The verses are:

> First Corinthians 16:1–3, "Now concerning the collection for the saints, as I have given orders to the churches of Galatia, so you must do also: On the first day of the week let each one of you lay something aside, storing up as he may prosper, that there be no collections when I come. And when I come, whomever you approve by letters I will send to bear your gift to Jerusalem."

These verses have been misused all too often to teach New Testament tithing; it is an irresponsible interpretation and unwarranted application. I discussed a similar "collection for the saints" earlier, at Acts 11:27–30. The Acts 11 prophecy occurred about AD 45 (Claudius reigned AD 41–54). First Corinthians was written about AD 57, about the time of Acts 19:22. In Acts 19 Paul is on his way to Jerusalem, and although Acts does not mention this particular financial aid to the Jerusalem church, it fits with Paul's trip to Jerusalem at this time.[14] A one-time financial gift to a troubled sister church is all there is to this passage. Paul was taking up a collection from the churches he had founded to support the financially troubled Jerusalem church. He requested any money the Corinthians might chose to donate be collected week by week, so that he would not be delayed by a collection during his brief stay. (Also, from a practical point of view, weekly collections might result in more donations.) Unlike the tithe, everyone was to give, "let each one of you." Perhaps a goodly amount could have been raised from the rich, but Christianity demands total dedication of self and possessions, and each is his brother's keeper. Each, therefore, was to contribute, as he was able (whether something small, middling, or large), to the gift.

The words "let each one of you lay something aside," are literally "let each of you put by him," and are reasonably interpreted as the individual setting aside an amount on the first day of the week. To "put by him" means the giver was to store the gift in his own home. The word translated "storing up" means "to store or treasure up goods for future use,"[15] more simply, to accumulate. Each individual was, on his own, to set aside something week

---

14. In 1 Corinthians 16:3 Paul says the church can send its own members to deliver the gift. In v. 4 he says he might accompany them. Since Paul is not said to have delivered the gift, Acts 21, the Corinthians must have delivered it.

15. Zodhiates, *Dictionary*, 735.

by week, accumulating it in his own home.[16] The translation "storing up as he" is literally, "storing up whatever," with "whatever" being the object of "prosper." The word translated "prosper," *euodoo*, was rare outside the Bible,[17] and means "success." The meaning in context is not yield or profit from gainful activities, which the English "prosper" implies. The meaning is success in gathering the gift, "gathering all that he can . . . The idea of success is linked with the result of gathering or saving."[18] The instruction is not "give as you have financially benefitted" but "be successful in gathering all you can for the gift." The intent of Paul's instruction was, "On the first of the week let each of you put by him [at home], accumulating whatever has been successfully gathered (saved) out of one's weekly income."[19] Each believer was to decide the portion he would save out of his weekly income, and set that amount aside, in order to successfully accumulate the gift ("prosper") week by week. Then, when Paul arrived, each believer would give him the whole amount he or she had gathered for the gift. The portion one might save out of each week's income was to be proportionate to income: whatever has been successfully saved. This implies that some may be able to save more than others.[20] Proportionate to income refers to the percentage of giving (the tithe required the same portion whether the crop was big or little). If one's income is little, giving is to be proportionately little, that is, a smaller percentage. If one's income is big, giving is to be proportionately big; a bigger percentage of the whole. There are two principles in 2 Corinthians 8:12, 13, discussed below, that help determine the proportion of income one is to give.[21]

---

16. Robertson and Plummer, *First Corinthians*, 384.

17. The only other New Testament uses are, Romans 1:10, "I may find a way," and 3 John 1, "prosper" (2X).

18. Kittel and Friedrich, *Dictionary*, 5:113–114.

19. Put another way, each is to set something aside, week by week, accumulating it as he may be successful in saving it.

20. Living expenses are relatively the same for everyone in a certain income group: poor, middle class, wealthy. The expenses of food, utilities, rent/mortgage, etc., are about the same as your neighbor's. If your job pays more, or less, than your neighbor (but not enough more or less to put you into another economic class) then you should be giving proportionate to the greater (or lesser) income, because you have more (or less) from which to successfully gather money for giving.

21. Giving is according to what one has, not according to what he does not have, and do not burden yourself financially.

The Tithe in Apostolic Times

Regular giving is a principle in the Old Testament. First Tithe was given after every harvest. Festival Tithe was given for each mandatory festival. A free-will offering, "as the Lord your God blesses you," was also part of the three mandatory festivals, Deuteronomy 16:10, 17. Sacrifices and offerings were given at the altar daily, weekly, and monthly. Paul drew lessons and applications from the Old Testament to develop principles of Christian giving for the New Testament church; he did not recommend a tithe. The tithe was a specified amount from a specified source. There is no tithe here. Everyone gives ("each of you"), giving is voluntary ("laying something aside"), regular ("on the first of the week"), proportional ("whatever you have gathered or saved"), and different for everyone ("as you are successful in gathering"). This is the way Christian brethren are to support one another.

The principles of New Testament giving in this passage are:

- Out of one's income each is to lay something aside, 1 Corinthians 16:2
- Give regularly, 1 Corinthians 16:2
- Give proportionate to income, 1 Corinthians 16:2

Second Corinthians 8:1–5; 11:8–9; Philippians 4:15–16

The verses are:

> Second Corinthians 8:1–5, "Moreover, brethren, we make known to you the grace of God bestowed on the churches of Macedonia: that in a great trial of affliction the abundance of their joy and their deep poverty abounded in the riches of their liberality. For I bear witness that according to their ability, yes, and beyond their ability, they were freely willing, imploring us with much urgency that we would receive the gift and the fellowship of the ministering to the saints. And not only as we had hoped, but they first gave themselves to the Lord, and then to us by the will of God."

> Second Corinthians 11:8–9, "I robbed other churches, taking wages from them to minister to you. And when I was present with you, and in need, I was a burden to no one, for what I lacked the brethren who came from Macedonia supplied. And in everything I kept myself from being burdensome to you, and so I will keep myself."

> Philippians 4:15-16, "Now you Philippians know also that in the beginning of the gospel, when I departed from Macedonia, no church shared with me concerning giving and receiving but you only. For even in Thessalonica you sent aid once and again for my necessities."

The first passage speaks of the generosity and sacrifice[22] of the Macedonian churches in sending Paul money to support his ministry in other churches. The second passage relates to the same issue, that is, the Macedonian churches supported Paul during his ministry at Corinth, so that he might minister the gospel without being a financial burden to the Corinthians. The third passage is Paul's personal thanks to the Philippian church for their support as he ministered to the Corinthians and the Thessalonians. As always in the apostolic epistles there is no mention of a tithe to guide their giving. In fact, the kind of sacrificial giving practiced here by the Macedonian churches is impossible under a tithing system, for a tithe is a legally obligated specified amount from a specified source. The actions of the Philippian church illustrate the teaching in 1 Corinthians 9: those who live of the gospel should live from the gospel, by reaping material things from sowing spiritual things.

The principles of New Testament giving in this passage are:

- Sacrificial giving is commendable, 2 Corinthians 8:2-3
- Giving is an offering to the Lord, 2 Corinthians 8:5

Second Corinthians 8:8-12

The verses are:

> Second Corinthians 8:8-12, "I speak not by commandment, but I am testing the sincerity of your love by the diligence of others. For you know the grace of our Lord Jesus Christ, that though He was rich, yet for your sakes He became poor, that you through His poverty might become rich. And in this I give advice: It is to your advantage not only to be doing what you began and were desiring to do a year ago; but now you also must complete the doing of it; that as there was a readiness to desire it, so there also may be a completion out of what you have. For if there is first a willing

---

22. For further comment on sacrificial giving see chapter six, heading "Sacrificial Giving."

mind, it is accepted according to what one has, and not according to what he does not have."

In vv. 8–11 Paul is exhorting the Corinthians to fulfill their commitment to give a financial gift to the Jerusalem church. When he says, "I speak not by commandment," he means he is not ordering them to give this gift. Rather, he is asking, What is the depth of your commitment; what is the practical outworking of grace and faith in your lives? Others gave diligently (vv. 1–4), will you be as diligent? The Corinthians were diligent in faith, speech, knowledge, and in their love for Paul. Would they be as diligent to fulfill their commitment to this gift? Was their love for Paul and other Christians sincere? Or had they promised but were now less inclined to their commitment?

The example of Jesus Christ, v. 9, is one of diligent commitment and willing generosity setting an ethical standard.[23] The argument is: Christ chose personal poverty (the incarnation) to help those in spiritual poverty (the unsaved). Could the Corinthians, who had become spiritually rich in Christ, act in faith by contributing generously to the poor saints in Jerusalem? Paul, v. 10, gives his advice: it would be to their (spiritual) advantage to see the collection for the Jerusalem saints through to its conclusion. As they had a "readiness of desire" at the beginning, so they must complete their commitment, v. 11, "out of what you have." The last phrase may mean they were to fulfill their commitment out of what they presently had on hand, or they were to continue to make a collection, 1 Corinthians 16:2, "accumulating whatever has been successfully saved out of one's weekly income."

In v. 12 Paul gives two principles of New Testament giving. The first is, giving is "of a willing mind." New Testament believers are exhorted to give, advised to give, and encouraged to give, but never commanded to give. For example, Romans 15:16; 2 Corinthians 9:7; Galatians 2:10; Ephesians 4:28; 1 Timothy 6:18. First Corinthians 9:14 seems to command giving, "The Lord has commanded that those who preach the gospel should live from the gospel." However, the idea of a commandment to give is an effect of the English translation. Paul is drawing out a principle from the Old Testament. Portions of the animal and food offerings belonged to the priests. For example, Leviticus 2:3, 10, "the rest of the grain offering shall be Aaron's and his sons"; "what is left of the

---

23. Compare Martin, *2 Corinthians*, 262–64.

grain offering shall be Aaron's and his sons"; 6:14, 18, "and the remainder of it [the grain offering] Aaron and his sons shall eat"; "all the males among the children of Aaron may eat it [grain offering]"; 6:26, 29, "the priest who offers it [the sin offering] for sin shall eat it"; "all the males among the priests may eat it [sin offering]"; 7:6, "every male among the priests may eat it [the trespass offering]"; 7:31, "the breast [of the peace offering] shall be Aaron's and his sons." We see from these examples that the Lord's commandment was that the priests were due a portion of the offerings from the altar. In some cases it was a commandment to the priests to eat their part of the offering (6:26), and in some cases it expressed what the priests were allowed to eat. The authorization (or commandment if you prefer) was not directed to the people giving the offering but to the priest sacrificing the offering. From this Old Testament principle (expressed at 1 Corinthians 9:13, "those who serve at the altar partake of the altar") Paul developed a precept applicable to the New Testament gospel ministers: "Even so the Lord has commanded that those who preach the gospel should live from the gospel." In other words, a portion from the gospel is due to those who live for the gospel. It is not a commandment to the givers to give—their giving is assumed. The discussion in 1 Corinthians 9:7–14 is not that the Corinthians should be giving to support gospel ministers. The discussion is who was qualified to receive their giving. Paul's answer is, everyone who ministers the gospel to the Corinthians is qualified to receive the Corinthians' giving as their means of support. The "commandment" is an authorization for the gospel worker to live from their labor at the gospel "altar." New Testament giving is voluntary, as is the decision to live from the gospel, 1 Corinthians 9:12, 15.

First Corinthians 9:14 is literally, "So also the Lord has appointed to those the gospel announcing of the gospel to live." The word translated "has commanded" in the NKJV is *diatasso*, used sixteen times in the New Testament, four of which are in 1 Corinthians. The word means to appoint, to set up an order, to arrange. In 7:17, Paul gave instructions ("so I 'ordain'" *diatasso*) concerning marriage that the churches were to follow. In 11:34 Paul will "set things in order" (*diatasso*) concerning the Lord's Supper. In 16:1 he refers to his instructions ("as I have 'given order'" *diatasso*) to the churches in Galatia to make a collection of money, and gives the same instructions to the Corinthians concerning their gift to the Jerusalem church. In 9:14 the Lord has ordained (*diatasso*, to set up an order or arrangement) that those who preach the gospel are to be supported by the gospel. The believer is not commanded to give, he is informed of his moral obligation to give.

There is no word in the Greek text corresponding to the translation "should" in the NKJV, NIV, and HCSB translations of 1 Corinthians 9:14 (NKJV: "should [live] from"; NIV: "should [receive] their"; HCSB: "should [earn] their"), or the translation "to get" in the NASB95 ("to get their"). The text is, "So also the Lord has appointed to those the gospel announcing of the gospel to live." The verb "to those [the gospel] announcing" is a present active participle indicating repeated action. The verb translated "to live" is a present infinitive active indicating repeated action. The sentence could be (and perhaps ought to be) translated, "So also the Lord did ordain [appoint, arrange] that those persons who continuously preach the gospel are to be continuously supported from the gospel." The emphasis is not so much on the giver as it is the gospel minister. Those whom Christ has chosen to minister the gospel are continuously qualified to live from the gospel because they continuously preach the gospel. Obviously there is a moral obligation to continuously give to those who continuously minister, because those who sow should reap, 1 Corinthians 9:11, 13, and those who reap are to support those who sow, 1 Corinthians 9:10. It is the entire passage, 1 Corinthians 9:7–14, that establishes the moral obligations of both giver and receiver. New Testament giving was and is voluntary. Just as the New Testament does not set a legal amount to give, it does not create or establish a legal obligation to give. The New Testament informs the believer of his moral obligation and expects him or her to act like an adult. The New Testament believer is an adult in God's household. He isn't commanded to give, like a child, he is informed of his moral responsibility and expected to fulfill that responsibility from a willing mind as a spiritually mature adult.

The second principle in 2 Corinthians 8:12 is drawn from Paul's statement, "if there is first a willing mind it is accepted according to what one has, not according to what he does not have." "The meaning is simply that the disposition [of the mind] is what God regards, and that disposition will be judged according to the resources at its command. A small gift may manifest in one case much greater willingness to give, than a much larger gift in another."[24] Paul was careful not to require the

---

24. Hodge, *2 Corinthians*, 204.

Corinthians to follow the Macedonian example, v. 3. The Macedonians' willingness to give was beyond their financial capability. One may make a choice to give beyond ability, but such giving is not the standard. The standard for giving is according to what one has, not according to what he does not have. That raises the question, how does one define "according to what one has"? How much should a willing disposition be disposed to give? The answer is not the same for New Testament giving as it was for tithing. The tither, because the tithe was food, always had an ability to give. His food was distributed ten percent to others and ninety percent for himself. No matter how much or how little food he produced, there was always ninety percent left over after the tithe. He could eat all of that ninety percent or sell some of it to the non-agrarian population. Even in tough times he at least had food for his family. However, New Testament giving is about giving money. The early Christians sold their possessions and gave the money to the apostles. The gift Paul would take to Jerusalem from the Corinthian church was money. Giving money is not the same as tithing food. The person who gives money is not creating money like the farmer creates food. His labor earns it, but that is not the same as growing food. Without exception the Old Testament farmer grew more food than needed for his tithes. Most of us, however, can earn only so much money, and sometimes the amount of money earned is less than the amount that is obligated to others. The tither in Israel was never in a position where one hundred percent of his food production belonged to another. Money can be obligated one hundred percent to others with none left over for self or giving. When one's personal economy is based on money, then money is needed to buy food, shelter, other necessities, and all things desired. The guideline, "not according to what he does not have," becomes relevant when giving is money.

Since giving is, "according to what one has," how much is, "what one has"? Paul's instructions in 1 Corinthians 16:2 gave the Corinthians guidance: "On the first of the week each of you lay by him, accumulating whatever [some amount for the gift] as you can successfully save." In context the instruction was to successfully gather an undefined amount out of their weekly income. "What one has," 2 Corinthians 8:12, is ideally total income from working in the world, out of which one gathers some (undefined) portion of income. How much were they to gather each week for the gift? In the very practical terms of living in the world, "what one has," is income minus necessary obligations. They were to give out of what they had after satisfying their necessary obligations. I believe this is what Paul meant in v. 13, "For I do not mean that others should be eased and you burdened" (see discussion on 2 Corinthians 8:13–15). If I am to give something out of what I have, then what I have is not everything I might receive, it is everything I have after obeying the biblical commands to satisfy my necessary obligations and debts. What sense is it to give so much to God out of my total income (the "give to God first," or "off the top" philosophy) if I am left with insufficient means to live in the world? Soon I would have nothing left to give to God. God does not give a moral obligation without also giving the means to satisfy it. "What one has," as a general principle of God's providence, is an amount to satisfy all lawful obligations and debts, including giving to support God's ministers and ministries.

The principles of New Testament giving in this passage are:

- Giving is not by commandment, 2 Corinthians 8:12
- Give from a willing mind, 2 Corinthians 8:12
- Giving is according to what one has, 2 Corinthians 8:12

Second Corinthians 8:13–15

The verses are:

> Second Corinthians 8:13–15, "For I do not mean that others should be eased and you burdened; but by an equality, that now at this time your abundance may supply their lack, that their abundance also may supply your lack—that there may be equality. As it is written, 'He who gathered much had nothing left over, and he who gathered little had no lack.'"

This passage begins earlier, in v. 10, where Paul references the collection for the saints that had begun "a year ago," 1 Corinthians 16:1. They must complete their task (support for the Jerusalem church), 2 Corinthians 8:11, cf. 9:5. The standard of giving is "a willing mind." If one has a willing disposition to give to the needs of others, then the gift is accepted according to what one has, not what he does not have. What is important is not the amount, per se, but the fact it is given willingly, voluntarily. This scarcely sounds like the Mosaic tithes, each of which required ten percent. The Law required that the amount prescribed must be given as prescribed. In Christianity, willingness is the standard, not the amount. One is reminded of the poor widow and her two cents, Matthew 12:42; Luke 21:2. When one is willing to give, then other principles help determine the amount: a liberal, generous, portion of what one has, but not more than what one does not have, and here is where v. 13 becomes applicable.

In v. 13, Paul says that the believer is not to give in a way that creates a financial burden. Verse 13 could be paraphrased, "Indeed, it is not a matter of relieving others at the expense of your own affliction."[25] One should not give so much that he creates financial problems for himself. Of the several principles of New Testament giving, which include liberally, generously, and bountifully (see below), giving is also completely voluntary. Therefore, no one is obligated to give God so much that he cannot meet his necessary and lawful debts in order to live in the world. The amount one is to give is not specified, but paying one's debts is emphasized in the New Testament. Certain obligations and debts are necessary to live in the world. I believe the principles of New Testament giving take all necessary obligations and debts into account by making giving "according to what one has, not according to what he does not have." God provides the believer an income gained from working in the world. In the course of God's general providence that income is sufficient to meet two necessary obligations: living in the world and supporting God's ministers and ministries. The abundance left after satisfying the necessities of living in the world should be used to support God's ministers and ministries. In every practical sense what one "does not have" for giving is the money God gives to satisfy the necessary obligations and debts caused by living in the world, and "what one has" for giving is the abundance one has after satisfying necessary obligations and debts. The general providence of God that gives a believer the income necessary to both live in the world and support God's ministers and ministries leads to one conclusion. To give so much as to injure one's ability to live in the world is to misuse what God has given; to give so little that one has an abundance beyond what is necessary to live in the world is to rob God.[26] The first is to give out of what one does not have; the second is to withhold what one does have.

25. Martin, *2 Corinthians*, 266.

26. Sometimes God gives more income than is needed to satisfy one's regular debts and giving. That money is God's generosity to be used for satisfying lawful desires or to increase support to his ministers and ministries. See the extended discussion in chapter six, section "How Much Should I Give."

The Tithe in Apostolic Times

There is also a principle of equity in Christian giving. Giving is a matter of *isotes*, being equitable, v. 14. At one time the Corinthian church received financial support, that is, Paul was supported financially by other churches as he ministered to the Corinthians. Now it was time for the Corinthians to support a sister church in financial need. Having been supported, v. 14, they should in turn do the equitable thing and support others. In context, the Corinthians were giving out of their (relative) abundance to the Jerusalem church, but in the future the circumstances might be reversed. The principle is, Christians who have something to give should share their material resources with those who are in need. To share equitably is New Testament giving.

In v. 15 Paul draws a simple principle from the Old Testament manna. God gave manna as daily "bread" for the people, Exodus 16:18. Every person gathered the manna according to his own need, the result being that God had supplied the abundance needed to meet every need. So too in Christianity: God can be trusted to supply every need. This saying is part of the moral law of sowing and reaping, Galatians 6:6–10. The Corinthians had at this time an abundance, supplied by God, out of which they might not merely meet their own needs but that of others. That would leave them with less but, like with the manna, God's providence ensured that the amount was sufficient for their needs. Therefore, share your abundance with others who are in need. Apparently, v. 20, the Corinthians gave abundantly.

The principles of New Testament giving in this passage are:

- Do not burden yourself financially, 2 Corinthians 8:13
- Share equitably, 2 Corinthians 8:14
- Give according to your abundance, 2 Corinthians 8:14, 15
- Trust in God's providence, 2 Corinthians 8:15

Second Corinthians 9:6–8, 13

The verses are:

> Second Corinthians 9:6–8, "But this I say: He who sows sparingly will also reap sparingly, and he who sows bountifully will also reap bountifully. So let each one give as he purposes in his heart, not grudgingly or of necessity; for God loves a cheerful giver. And God is able to make all grace abound toward you, that you, always

having all sufficiency in all things, may have an abundance for every good work."

Second Corinthians 9:13, "While, through the proof of this ministry, they glorify God for the obedience of your confession to the gospel of Christ, and for your liberal sharing with them and all men."

Paul's subject is still the financial gift the Corinthians have been preparing for about a year, v. 5. His thought is to give them yet another incentive to produce that which they had promised. He references the moral law of sowing and reaping, using an agricultural metaphor. "Bountifully" is not the standard of giving. "The issue is not the amount of the gift so much as the involvement it reflects."[27] The standard of giving, v. 7, is "as he purposes in his heart, not grudgingly [literally: 'not with sorrow'] or of necessity." The believer makes a moral decision to give[28] because the will of God requires him to give. A moral decision is not counter to thoughtfulness and joy in giving. One sees the need, is convicted by the Holy Spirit, and determines to give because doing God's will is his desire, his joy. The reason, doing God's will, means one's giving is not with sorrow (regret; unwilling to let the money go), or of necessity (as though pressured to give), but from delight; the righteous man delights himself in the will of God, Psalm 1:2; cf. 37:4; 40:8.

The word translated "cheerful" does mean joyfully, happily.[29] The phrase "God loves a cheerful giver," is explanatory of the phrase "not grudgingly or of necessity." "Cheerful" in context means happy in the sense of willingly, voluntarily. The point is not the sentiment of joy or happiness, but the inclination to act agreeable to God's will: voluntarily yielding the intent of the soul to the needs of others according to the will of God. The decision is to give eagerly, out of the desire to please God and submit to his will. The emotion happiness can accompany such an attitude, but the attitude, not the emotion, is the root to becoming a happy,

---

27. Martin, *2 Corinthians*, 289.

28. Ibid, 290.

29. Because the Greek is *hilaros*, which is a root of the English "hilarious," preachers sometimes recommend laughing all the way to the offering plate. However, "although the English word 'hilarious' is derived from *hilaros*, it does not at all convey its correct meaning. The word denotes a happy, glad or cheerful state of mind and not one overcome with laughter or mirth, or one humorously affected," Zodhiates, *Dictionary*, 768.

generous, willing giver. Giving is a delight because it is an honor and joy to give to God[30] by giving to meet the necessities of his people.

Verse 8 repeats a principle from 8:15: trust in God's providence. The first thought is that God gives the believer both the desire to give and the resources out of which he (or she) can give. The second thought is that in matters of finances, God makes the believer have a sufficiency that meets the needs in his or her life, which needs include the moral obligation to give. This doesn't mean there is no testing, no times of financial distress. If this were the case then why did the Jerusalem church need financial aid? Testing will occur, but no matter, one is to trust in God's providence to provide a sufficiency, either directly, or through others whom he is blessing with more. If Christians with more are following God's principles of giving by sharing equitably and liberally, then those who lack will be made sufficient. Verse 13 is another way of saying sow bountifully, but the unique point here is not reaping because one has sown, but that sharing liberally will cause others to see God's glory and the reality of Christian faith.

The principles of New Testament giving in this passage are:

- Giving is a matter of generosity, 2 Corinthians 9:5
- Sow bountifully to reap bountifully, 2 Corinthians 9:6
- Give proportionate to income, 2 Corinthians 9:6
- Give cheerfully, not grudgingly or of necessity, 2 Corinthians 9:7
- Trust in God's providence, 2 Corinthians 9:8
- Share liberally, 2 Corinthians 9:13

Galatians 3:24–25

Although a reference to either tithing or giving does not appear in Galatians, this passage bears on the subject of the tithe. In Galatians 3:19, Paul asks his readers, "What purpose then does the law serve?" He answers that the Law was added until Christ came. Before faith came, by which Paul means faith in Christ not in the works of the Law, the believer was kept under guard by the Law. He then says, v. 24, "The law was our tutor [NIV: 'put in charge'; HCSB: 'guardian'] to bring us to Christ, that we might be justified by faith." The word translated "tutor" is the Greek *paidagogus*.

---

30. Hodge, *Second Corinthians*, 220.

This term originally referred to a slave who was responsible to conduct children to and from school, thus he was the guardian of their moral and physical safety. Over time the word also came to mean a teacher, but the original meaning was not lost. The word *paidagogus* might be translated "supervisory guardian ... in antiquity a *paidagogus* was distinguished from a *didaskalos* ('teacher') and had custodial and disciplinary functions rather than educative or instructional ones."[31] Plato (427–347 BC), in *The Republic*, explained the *paidagogus* as "men who by age and experience are qualified to serve as both leaders and custodians of children."[32] Paul uses the term to describe the supervisory nature of the Law. Paul says, v. 25, "After faith has come, we are no longer under a *paidagogus*." The sense is temporal. Before Christ came the Law served as the guardian of faith and morals. Now that Christ has come the Law has completed its function and the believer is being kept by Christ. "No longer could it be argued that circumcision, Jewish dietary laws, following distinctly Jewish ethical precepts, or any other matter having to do with a Jewish lifestyle were requisites for the life of faith,"[33] and that includes tithing. "Now that the gospel revelation has been made, and believed by us, we stand no more in need of such an elementary, restrictive, external dispensation as the law."[34] The Law was "from its very nature temporary; it ceased when the faith came ... the coming of the object of that faith—Christ ... marks the period when the children pass from the austere constraint and tutelage of the law into maturity and freedom ... and the reason is, we are not children, but are now sons full-grown."[35] The tithe was the precept (rule) by which the Old Testament saints fulfilled God's priorities in giving: supporting those who function as full time ministers of the gospel; supporting the poor; providing the means of personal worship. The tithe, however, is neither a rule nor a model for Christian giving, because the gospel treats the believer an adult capable of making his or her own decisions regarding giving.

---

31. Longenecker, *Galatians*, 146.
32. Ibid.
33. Ibid, 149.
34. Brown, *Galatians*, 178.
35. Eadie, *Galatians*, 284.

The Tithe in Apostolic Times

Hebrews 7:2, 4, 5, 6, 8, 9

Because this is a long passage, I have listed here only those verses where the words tithe or tenth occur. The Greek words are *apodekatoo*, "to tithe from," *dekate*, "a tenth part," and *dekatoo*, "to give or take a tenth."

> v. 2, "to whom [Melchizedek] also Abraham gave a tenth [*dekate*] part of all, first being translated 'king of righteousness,' and then also king of Salem, meaning 'king of peace.'"
>
> v. 4, "Now consider how great this man was, to whom even the patriarch Abraham gave a tenth [*dekate*] of the spoils."
>
> v. 5, "And indeed those who are of the sons of Levi, who receive the priesthood, have a commandment to receive tithes [*apodekatoo*] from the people according to the law, that is, from their brethren, though they have come from the loins of Abraham."
>
> v. 6, "but he [Melchizedek] whose genealogy is not derived from them [the sons of Levi] received tithes [*dekatoo*] from Abraham and blessed him who had the promises."
>
> v. 8, "Here mortal men [the sons of Levi] receive tithes [*dekate*], but there he [Melchizedek] receives them, of whom it is witnessed that he lives."
>
> v. 9, "Even Levi, who receives tithes [*dekate*], paid tithes [*dekatoo*] through Abraham, so to speak."

The Writer's purpose in speaking of the tithe was to show that Christ has, as priest of the order of Melchizedek, a priesthood that is superior to the priesthood of the Mosaic Law. Because Christ's priesthood is superior, then the New Covenant in Christ is superior to the Law, and has in fact superseded the Law and all its requirements (including tithing).

Abraham's tithe to Melchizedek was, in part, recognition of the positional superiority of Melchizedek over Abraham. "The tithe is the Lord's," Leviticus 28:30, and the tithe was received by God in the person of his representatives: Melchizedek from Abraham; Levi from his brothers. The principle is, the one who received the tithe was positionally superior to the one giving the tithe, because the receiver is God's representative to the giver. In giving Melchizedek a tithe, the patriarch Abraham demonstrated that Melchizedek was his superior in their mutual relationship toward the Lord. Even though Abraham had the promises, Melchizedek represented the God who had made the promises to Abraham.

How can Levi be said to have given a tithe to Melchizedek, when the man Levi was three generations removed from Abraham (Isaac–Jacob–Levi), and the Aaronic priests were several generations removed when they began to receive tithes under the Mosaic Law? The doctrine here is that of representation.[36] In the biblical view Abraham was the representative of his descendants. Therefore, when Abraham paid a tithe to Melchizedek, those who were in his loins, both seminally and by representation, also tithed. One sees that the Writer recognizes the difficulty of this argument, for he says, "so to speak," that is, Levi did not pay the tithe directly, but might be said to have paid the tithe through his ancestor Abraham. Thus, in this doctrine, the priestly order of Levi is recognized to be positionally inferior to the priestly order of Melchizedek. When the Mosaic Law was instituted, the regulations concerning the tithe made the sons of Levi positionally superior to their brethren. The Writer's logic is inescapable: if Levi, out of whom came Israel's priestly order, tithed to Melchizedek through Abraham, then the Melchizedek order of priesthood, of which Christ is the sole representative, is intrinsically superior to that of the Aaronic priesthood in Levi. To apply this logic to New Testament giving: since Christ tithes to no one, as being a high priest superior to all others, then believers, who were in Christ's Loins, so to speak (Ephesians 1:4), when he became a priest after the order of Melchizedek (Psalm 110:4), tithe to no one. The Law, with all its requirements, including the tithe, was superseded by the New Covenant made by Christ.

First John 3:17

The verse is: "But whoever has this world's goods, and sees his brother in need, and shuts up his heart from him, how does the love of God abide in him." This verse reflects one of the three priorities in giving: to help the poor. It conforms to New Testament principles concerning giving in that no amount or procedure is described. Giving is left to the conscience and discretion of the giver.

---

36. The idea of family connections through multiple generations, of man's indebtedness to his past, and his responsibility to future generations, were cultural norms (cf. Guthrie, *Hebrews*, 159–60).

The Tithe in Apostolic Times

SUMMARY

Christian giving is not based on tithing. The Old Testament tithe is not a model, pattern, or example for Christian giving. One gives in proportion to his abundance, because in that abundance God has supplied enough for one's self and others. Because Christ has ordained that those who live for the gospel should live from the gospel, the believer is morally obligated to support those who live for the gospel. The standard of giving is a willing mind, a cheerful heart, as one purposes, according to the abundance God has given, according to what one has, liberally, or sacrificially, as circumstances require. The soldier is compensated by the state he serves; the farmer and shepherd share with the owner in the fruit of their labors; the sower shares with the one who reaps; the oxen eats some of the grain he has threshed. Likewise, those who receive spiritual benefits should supply the material needs of their ministers. What God gives is sufficient, 2 Corinthians 8:15; 9:8. Since Christ ordained that Christian giving would supply his ministers with material things, then what a local church gives should make the minister of the gospel materially sufficient. This requires each believer decide what he will give and perform that which he has promised. We should remember that giving is an offering to the Lord, received in the person of certain believers whom he has made responsible to minister his Word to others. Receiving that offering does not make the receiver positionally superior to the giver. In the New Testament church every believer is a priest because he is positionally in Jesus who is the high priest. All believers are equal in Christ in the New Covenant. If one believer were to give a tithe to another that tithe would destroy their equality in Christ and set up a new priesthood. New Testament giving is not tithing.

5

The Tithe in Post-Apostolic Times

OVERVIEW

IF THE TITHE, OR some model or principle or pattern of giving drawn from tithing, was important to the post-apostolic church, then there should be historical documentation in their writings. Tithing is seldom mentioned in the writings of the church in the first one hundred years or so following the death of the apostles. During the third century (AD 200–300) voluntary giving began to be compared unfavorably to tithing. In the fourth century tithing was recommended as a biblical means to support the church. Between AD 313–381 Christianity flourished under religious toleration and became united to the state.[1] In the following two hundred years Christianity grew to absorb the temporal power of the state, and the tithe became a state sponsored tax for religion.[2] This

---

1. In 313 Roman Emperor Constantine issued the Edict of Milan, a decree of toleration for all religions. Under the patronage of Constantine and his sons Christianity expanded throughout the Roman world. In AD 381 Emperor Theodosius issued a decree requiring all persons to subscribe to the Christian faith as defined by the Nicene Creed, ending toleration for pagan religions and effectively making Christianity the religion of the Roman Empire. See Cairns, *Christianity*, 28, 93, 119.

2. Between 381–590 the Roman Church became more involved in secular matters. In 452 Pope Leo I protected Rome against the Huns by persuading Attila to leave the city alone, and in 455 he persuaded the Vandals to limit the sack of Rome to two weeks, thus saving the city from destruction. In 494 pope Galasius I wrote that God gave religious and secular authority to the pope and king, but the pope's sacred power was more important, therefore rulers should submit to the pope. In the following one hundred years Rome experienced several barbarian invasions which led to the breakdown of civil authority. The Roman Catholic Church stepped into this vacuum and assumed the civil power of the Western Roman Empire; in modern terms Europe and Great Britain. The Roman Catholic Church was the effective religious and secular authority in Europe and Great Britain from 590–1517. See Cairns, *Christianity*, 118–24, 152, 159–63.

tithe-tax was given in the Old Testament way, not money but a tenth of agricultural product. The Christian principle of giving, so clearly stated by Paul in 1 Corinthians 9:7–14, was lost to the post-apostolic church, and those who lived for the gospel lived from the tithe. A thousand years later, in the Reformation era, two types of European churches emerged in relation to the tithe. The Lutheran and Anglican churches, and other new national churches formed during the Reformation, accepted their nation's tithe-tax as their chief means of financial support. Other churches, many from the Anabaptist tradition, were formed apart from the state-supported churches, and these did not receive a portion of the tithe-tax from their national governments. However, the members of these independent churches were required to pay the national tithe-tax supporting the state-sponsored church. In most instances these independent churches set up a tithe-like system within their churches for financial support. The early American churches followed the practice of their founding denomination. However, after the American Revolution, the "voluntary principle" of church support replaced both the tithe-tax and tithing within the churches. Eventually, however, beginning in the late 1800s, many American churches began to return to the tithe as a model or principle of giving to financially support their church. The modern era is a mix of many forms of financial support. Some European countries continue to support their national churches through a tithe-tax, while others collect and distribute the tithe-tax equally to all faiths. In America some churches insist on a tithe and some are more ambiguous about tithing, choosing instead to focus on stewardship. Churches in other parts of the world usually follow the pattern of their founding church (that is, the particular tradition brought by their missionary founders).

THE CHURCH FATHERS

We begin with historical documents from the early church (100–590) that reveal a progression toward tithing, which becomes a church doctrine in the Middle Ages (590–1517). Lightfoot's five volume *Apostolic Fathers*, which discusses the works of Clement of Rome, (35 BC–AD 101; bishop of Rome AD 92–101), Ignatius (AD 35–117), and Polycarp (AD 69–155), does not have a "tithe" entry in its index, nor does the Scripture index list an entry for 1 Corinthians 9:7–14.³ Discussion of this issue was not on the minds of these early church fathers.

Irenaeus (130–202) had this to say about tithing versus Christian giving: "inasmuch as the working of liberty is greater and more glorious than that obedience which is rendered in [a state of] slavery . . . for this reason did the Lord, instead of that (commandment), 'Thou shalt not commit adultery,' forbid even concupiscence; and instead of that which runs thus, 'Thou shalt not kill,' He prohibited anger; and instead of the law enjoining the giving of tithes, (He told us) to share all our possessions with the poor; and not to love our neighbors only, but even our enemies; and not merely to be liberal givers and bestowers, but even that we should present a gratuitous gift to those who take away our goods."⁴ In another place he wrote, "And for this reason [offerings to God] the Jews had indeed the tithes of their goods consecrated to God, but those who have received liberty [Christians] set aside all their possessions for the Lord's purposes, bestowing joyfully and freely not the less valuable portions of their property, since they have the hope of better things (hereafter); as that poor widow acted who cast all her living into the treasury of God."⁵ Irenaeus contrasts the partial commitment illustrated by the tithe to the total commitment of person and possessions required by Christ and willingly given by Christians. He does not commend the tithe as a means to support Christianity.

Clement of Alexandria (150–215) spoke of the laws concerning gleaning "as proclaiming the goodness and righteousness of God who dispenses food to all ungrudgingly."⁶ Of the tithe he wrote, "the tithes of the fruits and of the flocks taught piety towards the deity, and not covetously to grasp everything, but to communicate gifts of kindness to one's neighbors."⁷ In context, he was not recommending a tithe, or a principle of giving based on a tithe, but demonstrating how the Old Testament tithe taught spiritual lessons.

---

3. In Lightfoot's comments on Ignatius' letter to Polycarp, paragraph 6, there is a technical discussion of the Greek term translated term "soldier's pay" in 1 Corinthians 9:7. The discussion does not interact with the context of 9:7–14. See Lightfoot, *Apostolic Fathers*, 2:352.

4. Roberts and Donaldson, *Ante-Nicene Fathers*, 1:477.

5. Ibid, 1:485.

6. Roberts and Donaldson, *Ante-Nicene Fathers*, 2:366.

7. Ibid, 2:366.

The Tithe in Post-Apostolic Times

However, as time passed, a justification for tithing began to be developed. Both Cyprian (200–258) and Origen (185–254) taught that the Old Testament Levites were the prototype of the priests of the church. "The Levites were not to be burdened with any earthly duties; that is why they received tithes; even so that is the way it is today with the clergy; the priest should be completely free to devote himself exclusively to the service of God."[8] An expanding hierarchy was developing that would eventually add bishops, cardinals, and popes over pastors and rank pastors over church members. The principles of 1 Corinthians 9:7–14 were slowly being set aside.

Chrysostom (347–407), "Homily on Ephesians," in his comments on 2:10, speaks of tithes as necessary to good works, in relation to aiding the poor. He references Matthew 25:41 and the punishment due those who had not helped "the least of these." His comments were, "Woe to him, it is said, who doeth not alms [charitable giving to the poor]; and if this was the case under the Old Covenant, much more is it under the New. If, where the getting of wealth was allowed, and the enjoyment of it, and the care of it, there was such provision made for the succoring the poor, how much more in that Dispensation, where we are commanded to surrender all we have? For what did not they of old do? They gave tithes, and tithes again upon tithes for orphans, widows, and strangers; whereas some one was saying to me in astonishment at another, 'Why, such an one gives tithes.' What a load of disgrace does this expression imply, since what was not a matter of wonder with the Jews has come to be so in the case of the Christians? If there was danger then in omitting tithes, think how great it must be now."[9] Chrysostom was archbishop of Constantinople. His sermon views the Old Testament Poor Tithe as a model for Christian giving.

In his "Homily on Philippians" Chrysostom has some comments regarding support for those who preach the gospel. He says, "but the things which are demanded of us of necessity, and with compulsion, as though we were slaves, and against our wills, are laid down by us with much readiness, while such as are asked from willing minds, and as if from free men, are again deficient. I speak not against all, but against those who are behindhand with these supplies. For might not God have made

---

8. Vischer, *Tithing in the Early Church*, 27, quoting Cyprian, *Letters*, I; Origen, *Homilies in Joshua*, 17.3.

9. Schaff, *The Nicene and Post-Nicene Fathers, First Series*, 13:69.

these contributions compulsory? Yet He would not, for He has more care of you than of those whom you support. Wherefore He would not that you should contribute of necessity, since there is no recompense. And yet many of those who stand here are lower minded than the Jews. Consider how great things the Jews gave, tithes, first-fruits, tithes again, and again other tithes, and besides this thirteenths, and the shekel."[10] The Jews gave by compulsion, but Christians are to give freely and generously to support their pastors.

"The renunciation of possessions was becoming more and more unusual in the congregations"[11] as the church entered the fourth century, and the church fathers began to see the tithe as the minimum way to meet Christian obligations to the church and the poor. "Thus Augustine (354–430) asks: 'How much should be given to the poor?' He agrees that we may keep as much for ourselves as is necessary—indeed, even more than is necessary for maintaining our own needs, 'Let us therefore give a definite portion. How large a portion? A tenth . . . Scribes and Pharisees gave tithes; you, therefore, may not think you have done something great when you bring your bread to the poor—and yet this is hardly a thousandth part of your possessions. And yet I do not condemn this; do at least this much.'"[12] Augustine's comments on Luke 11:39 include the following, "And how did they [the Pharisees] give them? They tithed all they had, they took away a tenth of all their produce, and gave it. It is no easy matter to find a Christian who doth as much."[13]

As church financing began to shift toward tithing, "the payment of the tithes is once again demanded as though the validity of the Old Testament commandment had never been called into question."[14] Jerome (347–420), in his *Commentary on the Gospel of Matthew*, commenting on Matthew 22:21, wrote, "and give God what belongs to God, namely tithes, first fruits, contributions, and sacrifices, just as Christ paid the tax for himself and Peter and gave God what belongs to God by fulfilling the will of the Father."[15]

---

10. Ibid, 13:227.
11. Vischer, *Tithing in the Early Church*, 18.
12. Ibid, 18, quoting Augustine, Sermon 85.5.
13. Schaff, *Nicene and Post-Nicene Fathers, First Series*, 6:435.
14. Vischer, *Tithing in the Early Church*, 19.
15. Ibid, 19.

The Tithe in Post-Apostolic Times

The *Constitutions of the Holy Apostles* is a late fourth century compilation of various church teachings. Book eight addresses "Concerning Gifts, and Ordinations, and the Ecclesiastical Canons." Section XXX is titled, "The Same Apostle's Constitution Concerning First-fruits and Tithes," and reads, "I [supposedly the apostle Matthias] the same make a constitution in regard to first-fruits and tithes. Let all first-fruits be brought to the bishop, and to the presbyters, and to the deacons, for their maintenance; but let all the tithe be for the maintenance of the rest of the clergy, and of the virgins and widows, and of those under the trial of poverty.[16] For the first-fruits belong to the priests, and to those deacons that minister to them."[17] This is obviously an attempt to administrate the New Testament church according to the Old Testament order of priests and Levites. The "rest of the clergy" are deacons, deaconesses, readers, porters, and singers, see *Constitutions*, section XXVII.

The "apostolic" *Constitutions* are a window looking into church administration in the late fourth century, but they are invalid as a comment on Scripture, as seen in these comments, "Hear attentively now what was said formerly: oblations and tithes belong to Christ our High Priest, and to those who minister to Him. Tenths of salvation are the first letter of the name of Jesus . . . Those which were then first-fruits, and tithes, and offerings, and gifts, now are oblations, which are presented by holy bishops to the Lord God, through Jesus Christ, who has died for them. For these are your high priests, as the presbyters are your priests, and your present deacons instead of your Levites; as are also your readers, your singers, your porters, your deaconesses, your widows, your virgins, and your orphans: but He who is above all these is the High Priest." The genuine apostolic writings scrupulously avoid any connection between Old Testament tithing and New Testament giving. What the *Constitutions* do show (at least in relation to tithing) is the degradation of the church from the apostolic ideal.

The monk John Cassian (or Cassianus, 360–445) wrote concerning the practice of Lent,[18] "By the Law of Moses the command propounded

---

16. What these first-fruits and tithes consisted of is not described, but other church documents tell us tithes were food. Tithes were not regularly commuted into money until the mid-1800s.

17. Roberts and Donaldson, *Ante-Nicene Fathers*, 7:494.

18. Lent is a period of forty days leading to Easter during which some Christians practice a partial fast. The tradition dates to early Christianity. Eusebius (AD 260–340)

to all the people generally was this: 'Thou shalt offer to the Lord thy God thy tithes and firstfruits.' And so, while we are commanded to offer tithes of our substance and all our fruits, it is much more needful for us to offer tithes of our life and ordinary employments and actions, which certainly is clearly arranged for in the calculation of Lent."[19] He continues through several chapters linking tithing to the fasts required by Lent. He also wrote concerning how one Theonas became a monk. "As a young man Theonas came to the aged abbot John in order to give him a tenth of his income." After commending Theonas for "fulfilling the righteousness required by the old Law," Abbot John notes that the Old Testament saints were not satisfied to "give tithes of their earthly possessions; rather, they renounced all earthly possessions and presented themselves and their souls to God . . . When we bring God tithes of our possessions, we remain under the yoke of the Law and have not yet achieved the pinnacle of the gospel. If, however, we strictly conform our lives to the gospel, we will be rewarded not only with good things in this present life but also with a reward in the life to come."[20]

The Prolegomena to "The Book of Pastoral Rule, and Selected Epistles of Gregory the Great, Bishop of Rome," mentions tithing. Gregory the Great was pope from 590–604. By this time the church had begun to assume the administrative duties of a dying imperial Roman government. The Middle Ages, in which the Roman Catholic Church was the predominant ecclesiastical and political power, ran from 590–1517.[21] In the Prolegomena the editor of this particular edition of Gregory's Works (James Barmby) speaks of the work and writings of a sub-deacon, Peter, sent by Gregory to oversee the church-owned lands in Sicily. These lands were "cultivated by native peasants, called by Gregory *rustici*, or *coloni*, who enjoyed the fruit of their labor, subject only to customary dues to the lords of the land; in this case to the Roman See. The principal dues we

---

mentions a controversy concerning the length of a fast prior to Easter, *Ecclesiastical History*, book 5, chapter 24.

19. Schaff, *Nicene and Post-Nicene Fathers, Second Series*, 11:513.

20. Vischer, *Tithing in the Early Church*, 22, quoting Cassian from *Collations* 21:1–8.

21. Other end dates have been proposed, "1095, the beginning of the era of the Crusades; 1453, the fall of Constantinople; 1648, the Treaty of Westphalia . . . 1517 was chosen because the activities of Luther ushered in an era" in which the emphasis was on the church as a body of individual believers by personal faith in Jesus saved, versus the church as an institution, Cairns, *Christianity*, 159.

The Tithe in Post-Apostolic Times

find referred to were, in the first place, a kind of land-tax, called *burdatio*, and further, the tithe of all the produce, which might be paid in kind, but seems to have been often commuted for a money payment. Among the prevalent abuses which Gregory peremptorily required to be corrected were an excessive valuation of the tithe, irrespective of the correct price of corn, when a money equivalent was paid, and in other cases the use of measures of too large capacity, and extractions in various ways of more than was fairly due."[22] By the time of Gregory the church was being supported by tithes paid by tenants farming church-owned land.

"All these [historical] texts demonstrate that the economic needs of the church motivated the re-adoption of the Old Testament laws. As the number of professional clergy increased, the more necessary it became to answer the question of how they were to be supported. Paul had merely established the basic principle that they should not have to provide for themselves. The Old Testament commandment of the tithe, then, was a welcome biblical indication as to how this was to be done."[23] The insights of this commentator are not completely accurate. Paul had established more than a basic principle; he had established all the principles needed to financially support the New Testament church. Three hundred years after Paul the church had created its own problems. Paul's precise definition of those who should receive financial support from the church was broadened to include deacons, deaconesses, readers, singers, porters, and virgins. According to Paul, those who preached the gospel as a full time ministry (in our terms pastors) were to be supported by those to whom they ministered. Other positions, such as deacons and non-teaching elders, were wholly voluntary, that is, unpaid, in the view of the apostolic writings.[24] Support for the poor was an individual exercise, not specifically a church function. The earliest post-apostolic Christians aided the poor by following the pattern of Acts 6:3, distributing money, food, and clothing—given voluntarily—to the widows, orphans, and virgins without families.

---

22. Schaff and Wace, *Nicene and Post-Nicene Fathers, Second Series*, 12:viii.
23. Vischer, *Tithing in the Early Church*, 30.
24. The "elders who lead well" in 1 Timothy 5:17 are "those who labor hard in preaching and teaching." The early church met in homes, each "small group study" led by an elder, who may or may not have been a pastor-teacher. Pastor-teacher elders who lead well were due material compensation. Verse 18 shows Paul had material support at least partly in mind. Cf. Towner, *The Letters to Timothy and Titus*, 361–67; Mounce, *Pastoral Epistles*, 306–11.

Paul intended the church provide full time support only to those who ministered full time in spiritual things, the teaching elders (pastors) of the church. The poor were aided as the church had opportunity. The fourth century church added deacons and deaconesses to the list of persons to be supported, and created new supported positions, the readers, singers, and porters. A new level of church hierarchy, the bishop, who was added to the list of persons to be supported, was created based on Paul's use of two words to describe the office of pastor. The *episkopos*, a word meaning overseer, became the church bishop; the *presbuteros*, elder, became the local church pastor. The New Testament knows nothing of an ecclesiastical hierarchy, and Paul's instructions are sufficient for supporting the local church pastor and the poor. Everyone else—bishops, deacons, deaconesses, readers, singers, and porters—should have been, according to the apostolic writings, a volunteer.

HISTORIANS AND HISTORIES

Moving from historical documents to historians, in Schaff's *History of the Christian Church* we discover that tithing in the church had a beginning. Before Christianity became connected with the Roman Empire "the clergy had been entirely dependent on the voluntary contributions of the Christians, and the Christians were for the most part poor."[25] Under Constantine's (288–337) immediate successors, "the church . . . enjoyed positive observances for the sacred day, especially the regular attendance of public worship, frequent communion, and the payment of free-will offerings."[26] "Now [late fourth century, as the church merged with the state] they received a fixed income from the church funds and from imperial and municipal treasuries. To this was added the contribution of first-fruits and tithes, which, though not as yet legally enforced, arose as a voluntary custom at a very early period, and probably in churches of Jewish origin existed from the first, after the example of the Jewish law."[27]

In the Middle Ages support by tithe became a permanent solution to the church's financial needs. Pepin, by decree in 764, imposed the payment of tithes upon all the royal possessions. Charlemagne (Charles the Great), 768–814, extended the payment of tithes to all lands, and in 779

25. Schaff, *History*, 2:100.
26. Schaff, *History*, 3:382.
27. Schaff, *History*, 2:100.

made the obligation general by a capitulary [an ecclesiastical or civil law]. Charlemagne created a unified Holy Roman Empire under his kingly authority. He "was a firm believer in Christianity and a devout and regular worshiper in the church, 'going morning and evening, even after nightfall, besides attending mass.' He was very liberal to the clergy. He gave them tithes throughout the empire, appointed worthy bishops and abbots, endowed churches and built a splendid cathedral at Aix-la-Chapelle, in which he was buried."[28] The clergy "were supported by the income from landed estates, cathedral funds, and the annual tithes which were enacted after the precedent of the Mosaic Law.[29] The tithes were regarded as the minimum contribution for the maintenance of religion and the support of the poor. They were generally paid to the bishop, as the administrator of all ecclesiastical goods."[30] After Charlemagne died, tithing suffered a temporary decrease. Tithing returned when Otto I, AD 962, revived and consolidated the Holy Roman Empire under his authority, even deposing the current (corrupt) Pope, John XII, and installing his own man, Leo VIII, as pope. In 1049 Pope Leo IX held his first synod, where "the almost forgotten duty of the tithe was enjoined upon all Christians."[31]

"The eleventh and twelfth centuries were a busy time of church building. Clerical incomes varied fully as much in those days as they do now, if not more. The poorer German priests received from one-tenth to one-twentieth of the incomes of more fortunate rectors and canons ... The clergy depended for their maintenance chiefly upon the income from lands and the tithe. The theory was that the tenth belonged to the Church, 'for the earth is the Lord's and the fulness thereof.' The principle was extended to include the tithe of the fish-catch, the product of the chase [hunting], and the product of commerce."[32]

In the latter part of the Middle Ages not everyone agreed with tithing, but Roman Catholicism rebuilt the philosophical foundation. Aegidius Colonna (or Romanus), 1247–1316, defended the supremacy of papal temporal power. "In the second part of his tract, Aegidius proves that, in spite of Num 18:20, 21, and Luke 10:4, the Church has the right to possess

---

28. Schaff, *History*, 4:242.
29. That is, the tithe was ten percent of agricultural products—food, not money.
30. Ibid, 4:330.
31. Schaff, *History*, 5:13–14.
32. Ibid, 5:800. The product of commerce may have been goods or money; Schaff does not specify.

worldly goods. The Levites received cities. In fact, all temporal goods are under the control of the Church. As the soul rules the body, so the pope rules over all temporal matters. The tithe is a perpetual obligation. No one has a right to the possession of a single acre of ground or a vineyard without the Church's permission and unless he be baptized."[33]

In England, 1342, "Provision was made for the sick and needy through the monasteries, guilds and brotherhoods as well as by individual assistance and state collections. The care of the poor was in England regarded as one of the primary functions of the Church. Archbishop Stratford, 1342, ordered that a portion of the tithe should be invariably set apart for their needs."[34] In the mid 1300s John Wycliff (1320–1384) wrote in his essay *Civil Lordship*, "Tithes are an expedient to enable the priesthood to perform its mission. The New Testament does not make them a rule."[35]

Another source of post-apostolic history is Latourette's *History of Christianity*.

- Beginning in the fourth century, the church "devoted a tenth of one's increase to the widows, the poor, and strangers."[36]

- "In 585 a synod of Frankish [a German people group] prelates had asked for tithes to be regularized. Pepin the Short (764) gave tithes a legal status as a recognized tax, and Charlemagne, 768–814, further endorsed them. [He] perfected a system of tithes for the support of the bishops and the parish clergy."[37] Charlemagne needed the tithes because he had so greatly increased the number of clergy.

- In Western Europe, between 950–1350, "Support of the parish clergy was partly through tithes levied on the fruits of the field, on merchandise, and on handicrafts.[38] From the tithes not only

---

33. Schaff, *History*, 6:35.
34. Ibid, 6:748.
35. Ibid, 6:327–28.
36. Latourette, *History*, 1:213.
37. Ibid, 1:356.

38. A tithe on merchandise and handicrafts was almost certainly money, probably from the sale of these products. Otherwise the comment that tithes were used "for the maintenance and repair of parish buildings" makes no sense. Although the church had other sources of money (e.g., investment properties, inherited estates, payment for a special Mass, and indulgences), money slowly became a part of the tithe in order to support the expansion and maintenance of church properties.

were the clergy supported, but aid also came for the poor of the parish and for the maintenance and repair of parish buildings."[39]

- Pope Innocent III (1198–1216), "to strengthen and purify the Church ordered that tithes for the support of the Church be given precedence over all other taxes."[40]

- Commenting on English history, Latourette writes, "in 1714 . . . tithes continued to be enacted for the support of the Church of Ireland."[41]

- As part of the French Revolution, on August 4, 1789, "tithes were abolished, thus at once relieving the peasants of a burden which had taken about a twentieth of their produce, and depriving the Roman Catholic Church of one of its chief sources of revenue."[42]

- In England in 1836 (by an act of Parliament), "the tithe, a form of revenue for the Church [of England] which had come down from the Middle Ages and which had largely been paid in the produce of the soil, was increasingly irritating and was commuted to a rental to be paid in cash. In 1868 . . . the compulsory payment of local parish rates for maintenance of the church fabric was abolished and was made purely voluntary."[43]

David Benedict, in *A General History of the Baptist Denomination*, when speaking of the feudal system under which the Munster Anabaptists lived, circa 1525, comments, "To these innumerable evils must be added another innumerable mass brought in by popery. Tithes great and small . . ."[44] The Anabaptist Manifesto that came out of the Munster incident called for, article II, "that the laws of tithing in the Old Testament ought not to be enforced under the present economy, and praying that they may be allowed to pay the tithe of their corn, and be excused from paying any other; and that this may be divided by a committee into three equal parts, the first to be applied to the support of their teachers, the second to the relief of poor folks, and the third to the payment of such public taxes and

---

39. Latourette, *History*, 1:526.
40. Ibid, 1:484.
41. Latourette, *History*, 2:831.
42. Ibid, 2:1009.
43. Ibid, 2:1166.
44. Benedict, *Baptist History*, 1:229.

dues as had been exacted of people in mean [poor] circumstances." On the other hand, in Bangs' four volume *History of the Methodist Church*, which begins with the year 1766, the word "tithe" does not occur until volume four, where it is found in the pastoral address to the General Conference of 1840.[45]

CHURCH CREEDS AND STATEMENTS OF FAITH

Another source where one would expect to find some mention of tithing is the three volume *Creeds of Christendom*, by Philip Schaff. Beginning with Ignatius, AD 107, and continuing to 1925, Schaff gives about ninety doctrinal statements of the church or individual Christians, including discussion, commentary, and comparisons concerning these statements of faith. These creeds and statements of faith come from the earliest Christian writers, the seven ecumenical councils 325–787, Roman Catholic canons, councils, and encyclicals 1563–1928, Greek and Russian creeds 1643–1839, Lutheran churches 1529–1592, Evangelical Reformed churches 1523–1647, Congregational confessions 1658–1871, Baptist confessions 1688–1868, Presbyterian confessions 1655–1870, Quaker, Moravian, Methodist, Reformed Episcopal, and other confessions 1675–1846. Also included is discussion of various confessions and creeds from 1880–1925.

Tithing is not mentioned in these ninety documents. The word does not occur, the concept is not present, the Old Testament tithe is not used as an example or model or pattern for Christian giving. There are many reasons for this. The church began to be supported by government taxation (a tithe-tax), after Christianity became a state sponsored religion in 381. Other doctrinal issues were more importance to address in their creeds and statements of faith. In the Middle Ages the tithe-tax levied by the Roman church was considered by most people the normal means for church support, though often considered excessive. In the Reformation the newly formed denominations attached themselves to their various national entities and accepted a state tithe-tax for their support, eliminating the need to address financial support in their statements of faith. Only slowly, as certain denominations began to separate from the state, did the issue of financial support appear in the non-state churches' statements of

---

45. Bangs, *History of Methodist Church*, 4:378. The reference to tithes appears figurative of financial support, not literally tithes.

faith.[46] The same silence is reflected in the American churches, which began following the "voluntary principle" in the break with Great Britain, and formalized it with the ratification of the American Constitution in 1788. Although the means of financial support—tithing or giving money—is never mentioned in the ninety creeds and statements of faith complied by Schaff, mention of how financial resources were to be used is found in five statements of faith from churches after the Reformation.

- The French Confession, 1559, article XXIX, and the Belgic Confession, 1561, Article XXX, have statements concerning relieving the poor and those in affliction to distress, according to their necessities, but no statement is made as to how this is to be arranged or paid by the church.

- The thirty-eighth article of the thirty-nine articles of the Church of England, 1571, and the Irish articles of religion, 1615, address the issue of aid to the poor, "Notwithstanding every man ought of such things as he possesseth liberally to give alms to the poor, according to his ability." The subject here is aid to the poor as an individual exercise in giving. The thirty-nine articles do not address financial support for the church.

- The Westminster Confession of Faith, 1647, chapter XXVI, Of the Communion of Saints, section II, states, "Saints, by profession, are bound to maintain an holy fellowship and communion in the worship of God, and in performing such other spiritual services as tend to their mutual edification; as also relieving each other in outward things, according to their several abilities and necessities. Which communion, as God offereth opportunity, is to be extended unto all those who, in every place, call upon the name of the Lord Jesus." This statement commends aid to the poor as a Christian duty.

- The Savoy Declaration, 1658, article, Of the Institution of Churches and the Order Apointed [sic] in Them by Jesus Christ, section XIV, states, "... they who are engaged in the work of Public

---

46. The Dissenter churches, such as the Waldensians, Anabaptists (spiritual ancestors of today's Hutterites, Mennonites, and Amish), and Albigensians, were never part of the Roman Church. They paid the state tithe-tax, but did not receive the benefits. Current doctrinal statements and statements of faith do not address the manner of financial support in these churches.

Preaching, and enjoy the Public Maintenance upon that account . . ." and the section continues with certain duties required of those who enjoy "Public Maintenance." Public maintenance is not defined.

- The Baptist Confession of 1688 (also known as The Philadelphia Confession), article, Of the Church, section 10, states, "The work of pastors being constantly to attend the service of Christ in his churches, in the ministry of the Word and prayer, with watching for their souls, as they that must give an account to him, it is incumbent on the churches to whom they minister, not only to give them all due respect, but also to communicate to them of all their good things, according to their ability, so as they may have a comfortable supply, without being themselves entangled with secular affairs; and may also be capable of exercising hospitality toward others; and this is required by the law of nature, and by the express order of our Lord Jesus, who hath ordained that they that preach the gospel should live of the gospel." This is the only statement in the 1800+ years of creeds, confessions, and doctrinal statements reported in Schaff's *Creeds* that incorporates 1 Corinthians 9:14.

The absence of any statements concerning the mode of giving to support the church and its ministers (the "public maintenance" statement of the Savoy declaration being the only exception), is all the more amazing when one considers that most confessions of faith have one or more statements concerning the church, its ministers, its administration, Christian good works, and stewardship. One might have expected these confessions to indicate how "public maintenance" was to be obtained and equitably distributed. However, the most extensive statement on giving comes in 1688 in the Baptist (Philadelphia) Confession, a non-national church, that is, a church not supported by a national tithe-tax, but solely through church members' giving. Although this statement also does not address the mode of giving, it is the first and only statement of faith in Schaff's *Creeds* that uses 1 Corinthians 9:14 as the basis of its doctrine of church support.

The Tithe in Post-Apostolic Times

THE TITHE IN COLONIAL AND POST-COLONIAL AMERICA

The history of America reveals the change that occurred from a state supported church to what was called the "voluntary church." In the early history of the colonies "Virginia, New Hampshire, and Massachusetts promoted tax-supported churches."[47] Articles by "Virginia's Mother Church," 1631, included (old English updated): "Act XIV ... ministers ... shall be paid [an] allowance of 10 lb of tobacco and a bushel of corn ... Act XVI ... church wardens shall give notice to parishioners, that they bring in the duty of 10 lbs. of tobacco for the ministers ... the duty of a bushel of corn, be brought in upon the 19th day of December."[48] Parishioners were also ordered to "contribute towards the building of a church, or repairing of any decayed church [building]."[49] After the Catholic king Charles I was deposed in England, 1649, the Anglican church again rose in power. In America, in Maryland, a "tax was levied on all the colonists without distinction, for the support of the ministers of the Anglican Church."[50]

State support of the church and mandatory taxes or levies for ministers ceased shortly after the new American Constitution (ratified in 1788) was put into effect in March 1789.[51] In *The Voluntary Church*, editor Milton Powell has brought together eighteen letters written by European visitors to America between 1740–1860. The Europeans wondered how the state could exist without a state established and supported religion. They wondered how denominations and churches could continue without state support. With few exceptions these visitors found both church and state prospering. Unlike the European countries, many churches (many denominations) prospered side by side in the new world (several letter writers give lists of denominations seen during their travels).

William Corbett's letter was written during 1817–1818. He wrote, (emphasis Corbett's throughout), "I have talked to several farmers here about tithes in England; and they *laugh*. They seem not to believe what I say, when I tell them that the English farmer gives, and is compelled to give, the Parson a tenth part of his whole crop and of his fruit and milk

---

47. Leonard, *Early American Christianity*, 13.
48. Ibid, 62–63. (See also Benedict, *Baptist History*, 2:71ff.)
49. Ibid, 63.
50. Ibid, 109.
51. The change from state church to voluntary church was not immediate. Massachusetts was the last state to dissolve its ties with an official church, in 1833.

and eggs and calves and lambs and pigs and wool and honey. They cannot believe this ... But, my Botley [a city in England] neighbors, you will exclaim, 'No *tithes*! Why, then, there can be no *Churches* and no *Parsons*. The people must know nothing of God or Devil; and all must go to hell!' By no means, friends. Here are plenty of churches."[52] Corbett lists three each of Episcopal, Lutheran, and Presbyterian churches, and two Quaker and two Methodist churches, within six miles of where he was staying. "And, these, mind, not poor shabby Churches; but each of them larger and better built and far handsomer than Botley Church ... Oh No! Tithes are not necessary to promote *religion*."[53] He continues with an explanation of the individual church-goer. "The Parsons, in this country, are supported by those who choose to employ them. A man belongs to what congregation he pleases. He pays what is required by the rules of the congregation. And, if he thinks that it is not necessary for him to belong to any congregation, he pays nothing at all ... What need is there of tithes?"[54] In Corbett's England a tithe was demanded by the state and required of everyone, no matter if they attended the state church, another church, or no church. Not so in America. Corbett does not address how the individual church goer in America supported his or her local church without tithing, except to say it was according to "the rules of the congregation."

Not all reviews were approving. Many thought American religion vulgar, or on its way to ruin. A letter from Achille Murat,[55] who resided in America 1823–1832, mentions churches that "sell part of the pews." Renting (or "selling") pew space to parishioners, that is, renting certain pews in the sanctuary, was a practice brought from the old world as a way of raising money. In a later comment on the many religious societies in America Murat wrote, "it is only fair to add that these contributions [to various religious societies] are strictly voluntary," and remarks, "this explains ... How the vineyard of the Lord is so flourishing; it is by means of these immense sums extracted [by the many religious societies] from the pockets of the people." "There is certainly no clergy," he says, "so costly to the people as the American clergy ... [but] I have no right to complain, for no preacher ever received a cent from me."

---

52. Powell, *Voluntary Church*, 44.
53. Ibid, 44.
54. Ibid, 45.
55. Ibid, 53.

The Tithe in Post-Apostolic Times

Francis Grund, 1827–1837, wrote, "Churches in America are built [he means the building] when they are wanted, or whenever a congregation is sufficiently numerous and able to pay a preacher. With them the clergyman must be of more importance than the church [building], in the building of which they voluntarily tax themselves, without having recourse to the pecuniary assistance of others."[56] This will always keep the church poor; but I doubt whether the practice, while it lasts, does not actually benefit the people." [57] He notes that "every preacher is paid by his congregation" and "there is no accumulation of wealth" but "members of the clergy are, as nearly as possible, on a level with each other and those of private citizens."[58] He concludes, "the Americans, therefore, enjoy a threefold advantage [over the tithing system in Europe]: they have more preachers; they have more active preachers; they have cheaper preachers."[59]

HISTORIANS, THEOLOGIANS, AND PREACHERS

Observations made from silence are not always convincing, but the silence concerning a New Testament tithe is, as they say, deafening. Latourette's historical series *Christianity in a Revolutionary Age*, in volume IV, *The 20th Century in Europe*, has no mention of tithing in the index; neither does volume V, *The 20th Century Outside Europe*. Since his other works, including volume II in this series, do have a "tithe" entry in their respective indices, it may be a fair assumption that Latourette did not think tithing in the 20th century worthy of historical comment. The list of works where one might expect some mention of tithing, but does not find it, may be a testimony that some church theologians, historians, and preachers did not consider tithing a New Testament doctrine. The tithe is not found in Shedd's *History of Christian Doctrine* or Kelly's *Early Christian Doctrines*. The index of sermon texts in the *Complete Sermons of Martin Luther* does list one sermon where tithing is mentioned, Luke 18:12, but he says noth-

---

56. Grund does not mean a state tithe-tax, or a tax instituted by and required of all members of a local church, or a tax required by a denomination of its member churches, when he says "they voluntarily tax themselves." He means that the individual members of a local church voluntarily required of themselves a regular contribution toward building the church's facilities.
57. Powell, *Voluntary Church*, 76–77.
58. Ibid, 78.
59. Ibid, 80.

ing about tithing or giving. He has no sermons on 1 Corinthians 9:7–14, or 2 Corinthians 8, 9.

The index of sermon texts in *The Westminster Pulpit, the Preaching of G. Campbell Morgan*, does not list any sermons on 1 Corinthians 9; 16:1–4, or 2 Corinthians 9. There is a sermon on 2 Corinthians 8:7. The title of this sermon is *The Grace of Giving*. The subject was giving to support foreign missions, and specifically the London Missionary Society. The theme of the message was for the individual church member to give—not because he owed God a tithe, but because "the inspiration of giving must be the grace of God, the love of God."[60] Of tithing Morgan said, "I hear a great deal about the tithing of incomes. I have no sympathy with the movement at all. A tenth in the case of one man is meanness [that is, out of his poverty], and in the case of another man is it dishonesty [because he does not give in proportion to his wealth]. I know men today ... who have no business to give a tenth of their income to the work of God. They cannot afford it. I know other men who are giving one-tenth, and the nine-tenths they keep is doing harm to their souls ... Turning from principles, I want to say a few words about laws and regulations ... it is not that I am to give God a tenth or a part, and hold the rest to spend according to the dictates of my own desire. The Christian man must recognize that not a tenth, but ten-tenths, belong to God ... Out of my income I am to spend so much on food, clothing, shelter, mental culture, recreation, and all to the glory of God ... therefore, there must be a recognition of stewardship, and that means careful disbursement, not only of your hundreds and thousands, or millions, but of your pence and shillings."[61] In Morgan's view, "the grace of God to you is that He has put all His resources at your disposal. Your grace is to be manifested in that you put all your resources at His disposal. That is perfect fellowship."[62] Christian giving, in Morgan's view, answers the questions, "What does God want? What is his heart set upon?"[63]

Charles Spurgeon, in 3,561 sermons, never addressed tithing, according to the Subject index to his sermons.[64] He never preached a sermon on any of the verses in 1 Corinthians 9:7–14; 16:1–4; Leviticus 27:30–33;

---

60. Morgan, *Preaching*, 4:43.
61. Ibid, 4:40–41.
62. Ibid, 4:39.
63. Ibid, 4:44.
64. Spurgeon, *The C. H. Spurgeon Collection*.

The Tithe in Post-Apostolic Times

Numbers 18:21–32; Deuteronomy 12, 14, 26, or 1 Corinthians 16, according to the Exposition index and Scripture index to his sermons, except on 1 Corinthians 9:7. The subject of this sermon is not giving, but on being a Christian soldier. In his sermon introduction Spurgeon makes this one brief statement regarding giving.

> "The Apostle was proving that the minister who gives all his time to the preaching of the Word is entitled to a maintenance from those people amongst whom he labours. He gives divers illustrations, amongst them this—that the soldier who devotes himself to the service of his country is not expected to find his own equipment and his own rations, but he is provided for by his country. And so should it be, he teaches us, in the Church of God. The minister set apart to labour wholly in spiritual things should have temporal supplied found him. That isle topic, however, on which it would be superfluous for me to enlarge. Your convictions are so sound, and your practice so consistent, that you do not need to be exhorted, much less to be expostulated with on that matter."[65]

Spurgeon gave a short exposition of Genesis 14:17–24,[66] but the tithe was not discussed. Spurgeon gave two brief expositions of Malachi 3:8 and one from 3:10, saying,

> 3:8, "They had kept back from God's service the money which was needful for the carrying on of the worship of his house. We read, in Nehemiah xiii. 10, that 'the Levites and the singers, that did the work, were fled every one to his field,' for they could not live at Jerusalem, because 'the portions of the Levites had not been given them,' — their supply of provisions having been stopped through the meanness of the people who had thus robbed the Lord 'in tithes and offerings.'"[67]

---

65. Ibid, Metropolitan Tabernacle Pulpit, vol 62, sermon 3511, May 11, 1916, "The Battle of Life." The sentences "The minister set apart to labour wholly in spiritual things should have temporal supplied found him. That isle topic, however, on which it would be superfluous for me to enlarge," appear to have been wrongly transcribed. The words were probably, "should have the temporal supplied for him," and "that is a topic."

66. Ibid, Metropolitan Tabernacle Pulpit, vol 43, sermon 2523, November 8, 1885, "Abraham's Double Blessing." Spurgeon make this one comment concerning Abraham's tithe, "Abraham recognized the priest of God as his spiritual superior, 'and he gave him tithes of all.'"

67. Ibid, Metropolitan Tabernacle Pulpit, vol 52, sermon 2970, January 11, 1906, "God's Jewels."

3:8, "As to the Lord himself, if you have robbed him, attend to that business. 'Bring ye all the tithes into the storehouse.' Support his cause. Pay your fair proportion of the expenses of his house, and do not withhold that which is due."[68]

3:10, "They had kept themselves poor by their own meanness. If they had behaved rightly towards God, he would have enriched them with the bounties of his providence; the very windows of heaven would have been thrown open to give them abundance for all their needs."[69]

In the *Sword and Trowel*, Spurgeon's "newsletter," he speaks negatively of the tithe in connection with the state church. He occasionally mentions a tithe in connection with support of his various ministries, for example, the Orphanage.[70] In his work "Faith's Checkbook," in the devotion for April 24, Malachi 3:10, he wrote, "Let me give my Lord Jesus His tithe by helping the poor, and aiding His work, and then I shall prove His power to bless me on a large scale."[71] This statement seems to view the tithe not specifically as giving money, but as those good works that aid the poor and support the gospel ministry (which would include giving money). In my view, the negative uses of "tithe" in his works refers to the state's tithe-tax, and the positive uses are figurative: the people should regularly support God's ministries out of the abundance God gives them. I do not find positive evidence Spurgeon promoted a New Testament tithe as the means to financially support the church.

A survey of fifteen commentaries[72] on 1 Corinthians 9:7–14, from Calvin in 1546 to Martin in 1989, yields mixed results. Some view the passage as an extension of the subject of chapter eight, eating meat sacrificed to idols: restrict your liberty to eat such meat even as I [Paul] have restricted my liberty to receive support from the Corinthian church. Others view the passage in terms of Paul's authority to receive support. A few un-

68. Ibid, Metropolitan Tabernacle Pulpit, vol 36, sermon 2156, July 27, 1891, "Robbers of God."

69. Ibid, Metropolitan Tabernacle Pulpit, vol 52, sermon 2970, January 11, 1906, "God's Jewels."

70. Ibid, *Sword and Trowel*, 2:381, "if all believers who value the Institution will give the Lord his tithe in a conscientious manner."

71. Ibid, *Faith's Checkbook*.

72. Commentaries consulted were by Barnes, Calvin, Edwards, Godet, Henry, Hodge, Kelly, Lenski, Martin, Morgan, Morris, Poole, Robertson and Plummer, Ramsay, Vine. The commentaries are listed in the bibliography.

derstand the passage speaks of the Christian's obligation to support those who preach the gospel. A few indirectly mention the tithe in comments on v. 13 by referencing the appropriate verses in Leviticus, Numbers, and Deuteronomy. None recognize that Paul is developing a principle of giving that does not derive from the Old Testament tithe.

One would think that financial support would merit a line or two from the theologians of the church. The works cited below are from a broad spectrum of Protestant denominations. One of the earliest is Watson's *Body of Divinity*. To be fair, this work is a commentary on the Westminster Assembly Shorter Catechism. The Westminster Confession, on which the Catechism is based, only briefly addressed giving (see above) in chapter XXVI, but Watson does not address it at all. In the following works there is no index entry for tithe or stewardship, nor a discussion of 1 Corinthians 9:7–14: Hodge, *Systematic Theology*; Shedd, *Dogmatic Theology*; Berkhoff, *Systematic Theology*; Ryrie, *Biblical Theology of the New Testament*; Ladd *A Theology of the New Testament*; Marshall, *New Testament Theology*, Grudem, *Systematic Theology*.

Chafer's *Systematic Theology* has two entries.[73] "Stewardship is a New Testament doctrine governing benevolent giving and stands in sharp contrast to the Old Testament plan of tithing while equally different from mere random giving." In the entry on tithing Chafer refers the reader to his article on Stewardship, but also has this to say, "Tithing, or giving to God a tenth, is one practice antedating the law and still to this day [1947] a common usage . . . in contrast to Grace. Under grace, benevolence will function 'not of necessity' or because of any law requirement," and he cites 1 Corinthians 16:2; 2 Corinthians 9:7.

Buswell, *Systematic Theology*,[74] opens his section on "Tithing and Christian Stewardship," with "The giving of one tenth of one's income to the Lord's work is not explicitly mentioned in the New Testament, but the principle of systematic and proportionate giving is made quite clear." He cites 1 Corinthians 16:2; 2 Corinthians 9:6–9. Buswell attempts to draw an analogy from Malachi 3:10, the "storehouse." He states the word *thesaurizo*, translated "storing up" in 1 Corinthians 16:2, means "putting in the treasury," and this corresponds to the "storehouse" of Malachi 3:10. He also says that "Christian tithing" should be carried on not only to the

---

73. Chafer, *Systematic Theology*, 7:293, 304.
74. Buswell, *Systematic Theology*, 417–18.

local church, but also to Christian agencies that must be supported by voluntary giving. The plan of storehouse tithing (that is, to give money to one agency in order to distribute it to many others) "is by no means enjoined on the church." In regard to the word *thesaurizo* Buswell is almost correct. The word means "to store or treasure up goods for future use."[75] In the context of 1 Corinthians 16:2, in fact in the very words of that verse, each individual was on his own to set aside something week by week, storing up, *thesaurizo*, as he may be successful in gathering the gift. The word in context refers to accumulating the gift week by week, not the place the gift was stored. God's true "treasury" or "storehouse" is the individual believer, for God puts his money with his people by giving them employment and blessing their lives. The Christian in 1 Corinthians stored his collection in his home, not in a church building. When Paul arrived the church would not have to take collections (note the plural) to get a sum of money for the gift. Many collections would be required by the individual to accumulate money from several "pay days," thus Paul requested individuals *thesaurizo* their gift on a week by week basis. When Paul arrived the individual church members would bring out the money they had accumulated (*thesaurizo*) through their weekly collections from their income and give it to Paul.

Griffith Thomas, in his work *The Principles of Theology*, comments on voluntary giving as a means of aiding the poor. This work is a commentary on the thirty-nine articles (statements of church doctrine) of the Church of England. Article thirty-eight states, "The riches and goods of Christians are not common, as touching the right, title, and possession of the same, as certain Anabaptists do falsely boast. Notwithstanding, every man ought, of such things as he possesseth, liberally to give alms to the poor, according to his ability." His comments on this article that relate to the present discussion are as follows.[76] "There is no proof of it [Acts 2:44; 4:22] ever being required as of Divine or permanent obligation. It is obvious that everything was purely voluntary and not compulsory (Acts 5:4)." "The New Testament has three great principles of giving . . . (a) a man is to give according as God has prospered him (1 Cor 16:2); (b) he is to give according to his ability (Acts 11:29); (c) he is to give according to his heart's purpose (2 Corinthians 9:7)." "All the principles and methods of Christian

---

75. Zodhiates, *Dictionary*, 735.
76. Thomas, *Principles of Theology*, 481–82.

giving may be carefully studied from St. Paul's two chapters, 2 Corinthians 8; 9. It will be thus seen that giving is to be 'according to' (Greek: *kata*) not 'out of' (Greek: *ek*). A man may easily give a very small amount 'out of' his abundance, but this will not be Christian giving. He must give 'according to' his abundance, or whatever he has. The New Testament is thus true to its genius in avoiding all references to a specific proportion like the Old Testament rule of the tithe. In harmony with the essential feature of Christianity as a religion of principle, not of rule, it lays the burden upon the enlightened spiritual mind to give 'according to' what is possessed, pointing out that giving is one of the most definite and searching proofs of the reality of the Christian life (1 John 4:20, 21; 3:17, 18)." The subject of article thirty-eight is private property and "almsgiving" which is support for the poor, but it seems as though Thomas is promoting voluntary giving as a means of financially supporting the church. His "three great principles of [New Testament] giving" are applicable to every financial need of the church.

Gene Getz's work, *A Biblical Theology of Material Possessions*, speaks to Christian stewardship and briefly addresses the tithe. Getz, admits "the tithe system is never mentioned in the New Testament," but then advises, "today's Christians should consider this Old Testament model when determining their own giving patterns."[77] On 1 Corinthians 9:13–14 he makes this one comment without further explanation, "those who minister in the Word of God should be supported by the people they minister to."[78] Further explanation as to means and mode of support would have been helpful.

A tithe existed well into the 1800s in Europe, even where it was commuted to money. Today some countries still use a tax to support religion.[79] In America the "establishment" clause of the Constitution eliminated a state sponsored church system, requiring individual believers to voluntarily support their particular church. The voluntary principle of finan-

---

77. Getz, *A Biblical Theology of Material Possessions*, 113. In chapter six I address Getz's comment on the tithe as a model for New Testament giving.

78. Ibid, 207.

79. Today the Anglican Church of England is no longer directly supported by taxation. The church can (with the donor's permission) recover the income tax individuals pay on their donations to the church. The Lutheran Church is supported by a church tax in several European countries. However, in some of these countries new laws require church taxes to be distributed equally to many faiths and have made the church tax voluntary.

cial support for the churches struck down the compulsory tithing laws inherited from Europe. There is little evidence to suggest local churches and denominations promoted tithing as a doctrinal belief, or as the financial means whereby a local church, its denominational functionaries, its schools, or its missionaries, were to be supported.

THE MODERN CHURCH IN AMERICA

Modern church creeds and doctrinal statements are the descendants of earlier statements of faith, usually with only minor changes in words or meaning. In the modern age some denominations do and some do not include a statement on the financial means of church support.

The Southern Baptist Convention (SBC) *Baptist Faith and Message*,[80] article XIII, "Stewardship," states:

> "God is the source of all blessings, temporal and spiritual; all that we have and are we owe to Him. Christians have a spiritual debtorship to the whole world, a holy trusteeship in the gospel, and a binding stewardship in their possessions. They are therefore under obligation to serve Him with their time, talents, and material possessions; and should recognize all these as entrusted to them to use for the glory of God and for helping others. According to the scriptures, Christians should contribute of their means cheerfully, regularly, systematically, proportionately, and liberally for the advancement of the Redeemer's cause on earth. Genesis 14:20; Leviticus 27:30–32; Deuteronomy 8:18; Malachi 3:8–12; Matthew 6:1–4,19–21; 19:21; 23:23; 25:14–29; Luke 12:16–21,42; 16:1–13; Acts 2:44–47; 5:1–11; 17:24–25; 20:35; Romans 6:6–22; 12:1–2; 1 Corinthians 4:1–2; 6:19–20; 12; 16:1–4; 2 Corinthians 8–9; 12:15; Philippians 4:10–19; 1 Peter 1:18–19."

The article carefully avoids mentioning tithing, although it lists three Old Testament passages (Genesis 14:20; Leviticus 27:30–32; Malachi 3:8–12) and one gospel passage (Matthew 23:23) concerning the tithe. As discussed in chapter three the passage in Matthew does not support a New Testament tithe. Failure to include 1 Corinthians 9:7–14 is a significant omission.

The doctrinal statement of the General Association of Regular Baptist Churches (GARBC)[81] has no specific statement on financial support for

---

80. Accessed at http://www.sbc.net/bfm/, on March 20, 2009.
81. Accessed at http://www.garbc.org/news/?page_id=31, on March 20, 2009.

the local church. The following extract from article XIV, "The Church," is broad enough to include this issue. (Many Baptist denominations have a similar statement.)

> "We believe ... that each local church is the sole judge of the measure and method of its cooperation; that on all matters of membership, of polity, of government, of discipline, of benevolence, the will of the local church is final."

This statement leaves the individual church in this denomination free to determine its own philosophy and methods for financial support.

The Presbyterian Church USA[82] follows the Westminster Confession of Faith, 1647, chapter XXVI, *Of the Communion of Saints*, section II.

> "Saints, by profession, are bound to maintain an holy fellowship and communion in the worship of God, and in performing such other spiritual services as tend to their mutual edification; as also relieving each other in outward things, according to their several abilities and necessities. Which communion, as God offereth opportunity, is to be extended unto all those who, in every place, call upon the name of the Lord Jesus." The Confession references Acts 2:44–45; 11:29–30; Galatians 6:10; Hebrews 10:24; 1 John 3:17–18.

This statement seems to address aid to the poor ("as also relieving each other in outward things, according to their several abilities and necessities"), but says nothing significant as to means and methods to finance the church. The Westminster Confession was crafted at a time (1647) when the state (England) supported the church. This part of the Confession has not been updated to reflect the changing times and fortunes of this denomination.

The Episcopal Church states its official doctrine is the Apostles' Creed and the Nicene Creed, neither of which address how to financially support the church.[83] The Reformed Episcopal Church's position on giving is similar to the thirty-eighth article of the Anglican "Thirty-Nine Articles," quoted above, adding, "and as a steward of God, he should use his means and influence in promoting the cause of truth and righteous-

---

82. Accessed at http://www.pcusa.org, on March 20, 2009.

83. Accessed at http://www.episcopalchurch.org (go to Main Website Sections, click on Outline of Faith), on March 20, 2009.

ness, to the glory of God."[84] As was previously noted article thirty-eight of the Anglican confession addresses private property and aid to the poor. What one's "means" might be, and how to collect it, and whether financial support to the church is a right use of "means," are issues left undefined.

In the family of Lutheran denominations (eight denominations), there are no particular statements concerning the means of financial support. The exception is the negative statement of the Wisconsin, Evangelical Lutheran Synod, article VIII, "The Church and the State," section 7, "We reject any attempt on the part of the Church to seek financial assistance of the State in carrying out its saving purpose."[85] One would think that how to financially support the church should be as equally important as how not to support the church.

The Evangelical Free Church of America doesn't address the means of financial support for its churches.[86] Like the GARBC each member church is free to develop and implement any plan of giving.

The "Twenty-Five Articles of Religion" of the United Methodist Church, article XXIV, is similar to the previously mentioned article thirty-eight in the Anglican "Thirty-Nine Articles." Their confession of faith, article XV states, "All forms of property, whether private, corporate, or public, are to be held in solemn trust and used responsibly for human good under the sovereignty of God."[87] How this solemn trust is to be worked out in actual giving is not addressed.

Under the heading "Tithes and Offerings," of the "Doctrinal Teachings of the Apostolic Faith (Kansas)," Malachi 3:10 and Luke 11:42 are quoted without comment.[88] The doctrine of the "Apostolic Faith Bible College" states, without comment, the following "common doctrinal belief … A ministry supported by tithes and offerings."[89] Other Pentecostal-type churches have similar quotations, verse listings, or statements likewise given without comment.[90] Without their further comment it is impossible to know how these churches implement the Old Testament scriptures on

---

84. Melton, *American Religious Creeds*, 1:34.
85. Ibid, 1:39–161 (Wisconsin Synod, 1:160).
86. Ibid, 1:257–58.
87. Ibid, 1:261–66.
88. Melton, *American Religious Creeds*, 2:2.
89. Ibid, 2:3.
90. Ibid, 2:1–86.

tithing they reference in their doctrinal statements. Do church members give grain, fruit, nuts, oxen, cattle, sheep, and goats that the church's leadership later sells to local grocery stores? Or do the members commute their food tithes to money?

The articles of faith of the Baptist Bible Fellowship, article XX, "Of the Grace of Giving," begins by quoting 2 Corinthians 8:7. The article then states, "We are commanded to bring our gifts into the storehouse (common treasury of the church) upon the first day of the week," and cites 1 Corinthians 16:2, Leviticus 27:30, Malachi 3:10, and Acts 4:34–35, 37. Comments are (emphasis original), "Under grace we give, and do not pay, the tithe—'Abraham GAVE the tenth of the spoils'—Hebrews 7:2, 4—and this was four hundred years before the law, and is confirmed in the New Testament; Jesus said concerning the tithe, 'These you ought to have done'—Matt. 23:23. We are commanded to bring the tithe into the common treasury of the church. In the New Testament it [the storehouse in Malachi 3:10] was the common treasury of the church."[91]

The Baptist Bible Fellowship's article of faith conveniently ignores some facts. Abraham's tithe was, to put it in modern terms, from a bonus, not a paycheck. Abraham tithed from the spoils of victory, not from his regular earnings. By referencing Abraham's tithe does this denomination expect a tithe only from irregular sources? The "storehouse" in Malachi was several rooms in the temple set aside by Hezekiah to store food given in tithes, first fruits, and other offerings. Nowhere in the New Testament is the church ever called a storehouse; nor is it ever stated or implied that the church is a common treasury (see discussion above on Buswell). The New Testament churches did not have a building that could be a storehouse or common treasury, they did not have bank accounts, they did not have a church treasurer. The "storehouse" and "common treasury" of the New Testament church is the believer, because in Christianity believers are the church. When God wants money in his "common church treasury" he blesses his treasury—the individual believers—with money, and then convicts believers to give their money to church ministers and ministries according to their abundance. Finally, this Baptist Bible Fellowship article of faith requires their members to tithe, but what does tithe mean in a modern context? The problem with this type of "interpretation" is that it takes a culturally-determined action, in this case Old Testament agrarian

---

91. Ibid, 2:156–57.

Israel, and unthinkingly applies it to a different culture—New Testament Christianity.

Other Baptist-type denominations are more cautious, preferring, if they make a statement about giving, to focus on stewardship of one's possessions, such as the SBC statement on stewardship (above). For example, the General Association of General Baptists (GAGB), Statement of Faith, Article VI, "Christian Duties," section "F. Financial Stewardship," simply lists several verses without comment: "Matt 23:23; 1 Corinthians 16:2; 2 Corinthians 9:6–7."[92] It is a pity they did not include 1 Corinthians 9:7–14.

I could multiply examples from many faiths and denominations, but this is a fair sampling of Christian denominations and their approach to New Testament giving. Some reference a tithe; some focus on stewardship; others on social responsibility. None that I reviewed in Melton's *American Religious Creeds* (more than those listed in this chapter) used Paul's statement in 1 Corinthians 9:7–14.

---

92. Ibid, 2:186.

6

A Biblical Paradigm for New Testament Giving

THE NEW TESTAMENT GOSPEL minister, whether a pastor, missionary, evangelist, or some gospel ministry requiring full time dedication, is to focus on living for the gospel in order to be qualified to live from the gospel. This chapter, however, is not about the minister but financial supporters. Because gospel ministers are sowing spiritual things, they should reap material things from their fellow believers.

As the discussion now turns to focus on the principles of New Testament giving, one should bear in mind that, in relation to giving, there is a fundamental difference between Old Testament Israel and the New Testament church. Israel was a national entity. Israel had defined borders, a national government, and a national religion. The land of Israel was farmed by the people of Israel. Their tithes came from their land to benefit their nation. The New Testament church, in contrast, is a collection of individuals spiritually united to Christ and to one another, but physically scattered throughout the world with no permanent possessions, home, land, or government. The Christian is an expatriate of heaven, a foreigner living in a foreign land—the world—waiting to go home to his fatherland, which is heaven. He receives spiritual "care packages" from home, but must work in the world to make his way in the world. He supports Christ's ministers and ministries through his worldly earnings, trusting in Christ to supply a sufficiency for himself and the gospel. For the Jew, worldly possessions were part of his inheritance. He gave God a portion and lived in the world from the remainder. The Christian is not of the world, but he is in the world. Living in the world encompasses both material and spiritual needs. All his possessions—his income, his property, his very life—are provided by God as tools used to live in the world and support the gospel. This fundamental difference, between Israel in the world and the New Testament church in the world, accounts for the great difference in how Israel gave and how the New Testament church is to give.

PRINCIPLES FOR NEW TESTAMENT GIVING

Getz, in an otherwise helpful work, admits "the tithe system is never mentioned in the New Testament," but then he inexplicably advises, "today's Christians should consider this Old Testament model when determining their own giving patterns."[1] The tithe is not a model for New Testament giving. A "model," is a standard or example for imitation. The tithe as a model would be an example or pattern to guide or determine one's behavior under similar circumstances. The circumstances, however, are not at all similar. The Law exactly fixed one's religious, civil, and moral duties. When one had tithed he had given all he was required to give. Christ, however, challenges every believer to dedicate one hundred percent of his (or her) person and possessions to his service. The Christian's duty is defined by that total dedication of everything he is and all that he has. The tithe weakens and limits that challenge by fixing an amount a priori, implying that nothing more than a tithe is required. Accordingly, the New Testament does not set a rule for giving, nor an exact amount to give. As Griffith Thomas said, "The New Testament is thus true to its genius in avoiding all references to a specific proportion like the Old Testament rule of the tithe."[2]

The practices of Christianity are based on principles.[3] The practice of New Testament giving is not fixed by law but by principles. These principles make giving as limitless as "according to your abundance," and "trusting in God's providence," and as limited as "according to ability," and "not according to what one does not have" There are twenty-one principles, developed and explained in chapter four, that guide New Testament giving (in Scripture order):

---

1. Getz, *A Biblical Theology of Material Possessions*, 113.
2. Thomas, *Principles of Theology*, 482.
3. A principle is a fundamental truth of life. The manner in which a person lives his or her life is based on principles. From principles one develops precepts (rules for living) that provide direction in specific circumstances.

A Biblical Paradigm for New Testament Giving

1. Each gives according to his own ability, Acts 11:29
2. Out of one's income each is to lay something aside, 1 Corinthians 16:2
3. The laborer is worthy of his wages, 1 Corinthians 9:7–9; 1 Timothy 5:18
4. Those who reap support those who sow, 1 Corinthians 9:10
5. Those who sow spiritual things should reap material things, 1 Corinthians 9:11
6. Give regularly, 1 Corinthians 9:13, 16:2
7. Those who live for the gospel should live from the gospel, 1 Corinthians 9:14
8. Give proportionate to income, 1 Corinthians 16:2; 2 Corinthians 9:6
9. Sacrificial giving is commendable, 2 Corinthians 8:2–3
10. Giving is an offering to the Lord, 2 Corinthians 8:5
11. Giving is not by commandment, 2 Corinthians 8:8–11
12. Give from a willing mind, 2 Corinthians 8:12
13. Giving is according to what one has, 2 Corinthians 8:12
14. Do not burden yourself financially, 2 Corinthians 8:13
15. Give according to your abundance, 2 Corinthians 8:14, 15
16. Share equitably, 2 Corinthians 8:14
17. Trust in God's providence, 2 Corinthians 8:15; 9:8
18. Giving is a matter of generosity, 2 Corinthians 9:5
19. Sow bountifully to reap bountifully, 2 Corinthians 9:6
20. Give cheerfully, not grudgingly or of necessity, 2 Corinthians 9:7
21. Share liberally, 2 Corinthians 9:13

By following these principles the believer can meet his obligations in the world and to the church.

WHAT THE OLD TESTAMENT TITHE TEACHES ABOUT NEW TESTAMENT GIVING

Christianity can learn from the Old Testament tithe. The tithe shows God's emphasis (priorities) concerning the use of material possessions above what is required to live in the world. God's system of worship is to be supported; the believer is to provide for his own worship needs; the poor are to be helped.

The First Priority in Giving

When considering the first priority, supporting God's system of worship, one must be a careful observer and critical thinker. The observation is that the tithe supported the people who managed the worship system. The critical thinking is that the building (first the tabernacle and later the temple) was never supported by the tithe. Everything concerning worship (other than food for the priests and Levites) required donations not tithes. For example, oil, wood, and money were donated for lamps, the altar, charity, and building maintenance. The materials for Solomon's magnificent temple, and payment for the twenty years of labor that built it, came from taxes, not the tithe, 1 Kings 12:4.

New Testament believers are to support a gospel minister, whom Paul defines (for the purposes of financial support) as one who preaches the gospel so as to live from the gospel, meaning, the gospel minister focuses his time and energy on gospel ministry, not secular employment.[4] Supporting a building is not a requirement of Christian giving. A permanent facility for Christian activities is a convenience; in some countries Christians meet in the open air, or in member's homes. If, as in more developed countries, the concept of Christian worship demands a building, the first scriptural priority is still the pastor, not the building. When Christians add a building to their list of obligations they have obligated themselves to give above the needs of their pastor(s) who lives for and from the gospel.

The same principle guides the Christian obligation to those persons known as "staff." These persons are not Levites. The Christian church does

---

4. Bivocational pastors—those who work secular jobs to support preaching the gospel—are a reality of living in the world. A church's first responsibility in such circumstances is to evangelize and grow and give so that the pastor can focus on preaching the gospel and shepherding the church.

A Biblical Paradigm for New Testament Giving

not have a specialized Levite-type group of people to attend to the needs of pastors and buildings. This is because every believer, not just staff, is responsible to support their local church ministry. "Staff" do not preach the gospel, and the principle is that financial support goes first to those who preach the gospel as their living. God's three priorities in financial giving do not include "staff." Church staff, if not volunteers, are supported *in addition* to the three priorities. What about local church deacons, or elders who may rule but are not pastor-teachers? These do not make their living from the Gospel, therefore they should not receive payment for their voluntary work.

What about other Christian ministries? Some denominations employ bishops to be responsible for several local church pastors, archbishops over bishops, cardinals over archbishops, and so on. Each level of organization has financial needs. What about workers at denominational headquarters? My state denominational headquarters has fifteen paid staff positions, from "Director of Church Development Resources," to administrative assistant, to bookkeeper, to "Director of Finance," to "Native American Consultant," to "Director of Women's Resources." The church as the body of Christ has developed mission boards, denominational headquarters, para-church organizations, television and radio "churches," and many other ministries that do not originate and function in a local church. Each wants to be supported by financial giving from the local church. These types of ministries have been made part of gospel ministry, but they are not in and of the local church. The support of these types of ministries and ecclesiastical functions is in addition to supporting those who sow spiritual things to their congregations. I am not saying support of other ministries is not important, because the churches are to have an evangelistic outreach beyond their local area, Matthew 28:19, "Go . . . make disciples of all nations." That outreach may require an organizational structure larger and more complex than the local church. Local churches may choose to participate in these ministries so the church as the body of Christ can fulfill its function in the world. However, the church Paul had in mind in First and Second Corinthians was the local church. The first priority in giving is to support the local church: the pastor(s), church members, and the poor.

I have emphasized the local church because the New Testament emphasizes the local church. The Greek word *ecclesia*, which means a called-out group, or an assembly, is used 114 times in the New Testament. Three times, Acts 19, it refers to a group of Gentiles assembled to bring a legal charge against Paul. Twenty-two times it refers to all the local churches viewed as one body in Christ. Eighty-nine times *ecclesia* refers to a local church or a group of local churches. The New Testament emphasis is on the local church. The first priority in giving is local—to the pastors, for the members, to the poor—and then outward to other needs and ministries. Does the local church need to reach outward as well as inward? Yes, but they are to do so according to biblical principles and priorities.

The Second Priority in Giving

In order of frequency, but not necessarily in order of importance, the second priority in the Old Testament system of tithes was the Festival Tithe. The festivals, in modern terms, were a three-times-a-year religious convention attended by most of God's people.[5] God wanted everyone to afford to come. He wanted everyone to have a good time, Deuteronomy 14:26. The believer is commanded to come and worship, but God wants willing, joyous, eager, passionate worship. Therefore, it is important that a portion of the believer's giving be dedicated to worship. Perhaps that portion helps the church put seating in the sanctuary, fix the air conditioning (or heater), purchase hymnbooks (or permissions to use songs), build or repair needed facilities, run a van or bus ministry, and so on. Perhaps it buys doughnuts and cupcakes for the Sunday School class, or supplies ministry for women, children, or seniors. A believer may need a new Bible, a new suit, or a new pair of jeans to attend services; new glasses to see the preacher; or a new hearing aid to hear the sermon. However seemingly trivial or important, a small part of one's giving should be to support personal worship.

The Third Priority in Giving

The third priority, in order of frequency, but not necessarily in order of importance, is helping the poor. The tithe for the poor worked with gleaning to feed the poor all year long. Today we have no gleaning—picking food out of garbage cans is not gleaning. We have no national law or

---

5. The males were required to attend, but if the husband left the farm or ranch for a week-long religious retreat in a distant location (everyone walked, thus time and distance were related), it is a sure bet that, in the majority of cases, his wife and kids accompanied him—were not left home alone and defenseless. See Luke 2:44.

A Biblical Paradigm for New Testament Giving

custom of giving food to our city elders to feed the poor. But we do have means, many means in developed countries, to feed and shelter the poor.

The order of the "types" of poor in the tithing regulation is not an order of priority for assistance. The three groups of poor listed (applicable to the New Testament church) were the stranger, the fatherless, and the widow.[6] The widow was in desperate circumstances. In the Greco-Roman world of New Testament times a woman could not own property. If her husband died, and she had no male relatives or adult male children who could, or would, care for her, she was literally penniless and quite possibly homeless. Her economic choices were the kindness of strangers, a series of temporary and hard to find menial jobs, begging, stealing, prostitution, or slavery. The tithe was part of God's welfare system for the poor in ancient Israel. In these New Testament times a portion of one's giving should go to the widows, orphans and strangers who have no sufficient means of support. Giving should begin in one's family, then one's church, then society.

The fatherless were not necessarily orphans. They could be the minor children of a widow. Fatherless children were in the same economic distress as the widow, and had the same options. In modern society, especially western society, little children are valued in and of themselves, and for the assumed contribution they will add to society as the adults they will become. In ancient society little children were not valued. They knew nothing, influenced nothing, gained nothing, and could not be used for anything that could create value. They were little in size, thus in ability, maturity, influence, and profit. There were no orphanages, adoption agencies, or child welfare agencies. These things exist today because of Christianity, and are a means to help the fatherless. Giving should begin in one's family, then one's church, then society.

The stranger in Israel was not part of the family. He was a foreigner: a businessman; an employee; a slave; a beggar. If he was in need then he was to be helped. It did not matter that he was not part of the family, was living on the edge of society, was poor and needy, an irregular person no one wanted to know or meet. Giving the poor food or clothing, or shelter, as may be required, can be done through an agency, or personally, as one has opportunity. Poor Tithe was stored in the villages for the village elders to distribute to those who had needs. Your local church, or local "Rescue

---

6. There are no Levites in the gates of the New Testament church.

Mission," or other some city-county-state-federal organization, can act as your local village elders to help the poor.

For several years I attended an inner city church, literally down the block from the intersection where the prostitutes and drug dealers did their business. Many came to the church building for money, food, clothing, or other assistance. We helped each as we could. We didn't always "charge" them for our help with an evangelistic message; sometimes all that is needful is kindness and aid. A word of caution, never give money to persons living on the street, because money can be exchanged for many unsavory things. Give food or clothing. Once we gave pots and pans to help a single parent. Once we drove parents to the county welfare building, and back to their rented apartment, to help them get food stamps and other assistance. Even the firm rule about money may be broken under special circumstances. Once we bought a young man a bus ticket home to his mother (she had called the church; we physically put him on the bus), and gave him a little money for food along the way. Jesus said, Mark 14:7, "You have the poor with you always, and whenever you wish you may do them good." Under the rules of the tithe doing good to the poor occurred on a regular basis; regular giving is a New Testament principle. The policy of the apostles, and thus the policy of the churches they founded, was to "remember the poor," Galatians 2:10. Helping the poor is one of God's priorities and therefore a New Testament obligation. Giving should begin in one's family, then one's church, then society.

HOW MUCH SHOULD A CHRISTIAN GIVE?

How does the individual Christian determine an amount he or she is to give? The New Testament does not state an amount, leaving it to the spiritual maturity and conviction of the believer. The New Testament provides twenty-one principles of giving, which the believer is to work out in precepts (rules for living) that fit his circumstances and opportunities to give. The New Testament provides examples of giving, which the believer is to use as a guide. Some believers may desire more specific answers. My first response is that Christians are members together in a super-natural religion. Therefore, ask God the Holy Spirit for conviction—pray about it, listen for answers. Second, meditate on Scripture. Think about the principles of New Testament giving: what they mean; how they can be applied; how they fit into one's Christian life. Third, ask the counsel of more mature

A Biblical Paradigm for New Testament Giving

believers who believe in, understand, and practice New Testament giving. Decide on an amount and be faithful to it. Don't let testing stop you, for God always allows one's faith to be tested so that it may be approved and improved. Be willing to adjust as financial circumstances change, for ill or for good.

If all these helps do not provide an answer, then select an amount that fits your income (1 Corinthians 16:2; 2 Corinthians 9:6), and adjust up or down (2 Corinthians 8:14, 15), as required by your financial circumstances (2 Corinthians 8:12, 13) and the needs of your pastor and church (1 Corinthians 9:14). Be sure to give regularly (1 Corinthians 9:13; 16:2) and willingly (2 Corinthians 8:12; 9:7). Trust in God to provide (2 Corinthians 8:15; 9:8), and don't be afraid to give generously (2 Corinthians 9:5–7, 13), and sometimes sacrificially (1 Corinthians 8:1–5).

Sometimes wrong advice is given: under the Law they gave ten percent, but Christians should give more because (select one): Christians are under grace; Christians owe more because forgiven more; Christians have a greater privilege. That illogic simply establishes another rule. It sets an amount, ten percent or more, and therefore places the believer back under the Law. Neither Christ nor the apostles ever said the believer owes more because he is under grace; just the opposite, grace sets the believer free from the demands of the Law.[7] The New Testament teaches that the believer's person and all his possessions belong to the Lord. The principle is that all is available to the Lord, not that more must be given to the Lord. One might chose to give more to the Lord, or less, but that is the personal choice grace allows: each gives of a willing mind according to his own ability. The New Testament does not—never, no never—establish a rule stating how much to give. To "give more because under grace" is a rule: give more than the Mosaic tithe. No, you are to give according to New Testament Scripture principles. The believer has been set free from the Law by grace, not to be enslaved by a new law, but to live as a spiritually mature adult by grace.

Do not use the Old Testament tithe as the rule of giving, because that rule was for a different people under a different covenant living in a different historical-cultural time. The Old Testament does not provide

---

7. The purpose of the Law for New Testament believers is to remind them their moral duty and excite them to passionately pursue holiness, integrity, and faithfulness. The Law reminds us that we are to support God's ministers of the gospel. How we support them is not by the Law but by the New Testament principles of giving.

much help in answering the question, How much to give? We know that when the tithing regulations were given the number of adult males in Israel, not counting the tribe of Levi, was 603,550 persons, Numbers 1:3, 46. However, this does not tell us how many were qualified to be tithers, which required one to be both head of household and farmer. We know there were 8,580 Levites qualified to serve in the temple, Numbers 4:34–35, 46–48. Let us assume, for illustration purposes only, that ten percent of the population, 60,355 persons, were qualified to be tithers of agricultural produce. Let us assume each farmer reaped ten bushels of wheat. Their tithe individually would be one bushel, collectively 60,355 bushels, which would be tithed to 8,580 Levites. Each farmer would retain nine bushels and each Levite would receive seven bushels (out of which he would make a tithe to the priests of 7/10 of a bushel). In this admittedly imaginative example the Levite standard of living would be a little less than the collective average of the Israelite farmers (but he had a little land to raise animals). The more qualified farmer-tithers there were in the population, the greater the standard of living for the Levites. If twenty percent of the population were qualified farmer-tithers, then each of the 8,580 Levites would receive (using the same parameters as before) fourteen bushels of wheat. As discussed, Israel's economy was primarily agricultural, so the proportion of tithers to non-tithers was greater than fifty percent of the population. Under these circumstances the pantries of Levites and priests (and farmers) would be well stocked, even if some potential tithers were unwilling or unable to tithe. Those pantries needed to be well stocked, because unlike Christian giving, which occurs on a weekly or monthly basis (paycheck to paycheck, 1 Corinthians 16:2), there were no harvests, and therefore no tithes, from mid-November to mid-March.

Tithing food is not the same as tithing money. Using First Tithe as a model let us example a church in the United States in which there are thirty families. Let us make the net annual income of each family $25,000, and apply the ten percent rule. Individual giving would be $2,500 annually. If that tithe of $2,500 is used according to the Old Testament rule, then the pastor of that church would have an annual income of $75,000 ($2,500 X 30), because First Tithe supported the minister and nothing else. That is a fortunate pastor indeed, to earn three times more than the members of his poorer congregation. However, that is not how the modern "tithe" works. The $75,000 would be divided between pastoral support, building utilities and maintenance, and the whole host of church

A Biblical Paradigm for New Testament Giving

ministries inside and outside the local church. A church of 30 families needs an annual budget of about $90,000 to fund itself and support a few ministries outside their church. Under the modern rules of the new tithe (money only) and the needs of expanded church obligations everyone must give more to support more.

Under grace, however, each local church member is free to decide what he will, or will not, support. This difference, between a legal requirement to give and the individual under grace deciding what to support, is why New Testament giving was abandoned and Old Testament tithing adopted into the church in the fourth century. Ministries and ministers grew larger than the needs of the local church. However, the tithe, then and for 1,500 years afterwards, was mainly food (farmers) and a small amount of money (merchants, tradesmen, artisans), and therefore the burden was bearable. Today, those who demand a tithe from church members want only money.

The Old Testament farmer comfortably fed himself and his family out of what remained after First, Festival, and Poor Tithes. Let us imagine a farmer who grows only wheat, harvested in May, and barley, harvested in April. Let us suppose the wheat harvest is one hundred bushels. First Tithe leaves him with ninety. Festival Tithe in May-June (Pentecost) leaves him with eighty-one bushels. Festival Tithe in September-October (Tabernacles) leaves him with seventy-three bushels. Therefore, from May to April our farmer has seventy-three bushels of wheat to eat and sell. Let us suppose our farmer ate two bushels of his wheat in each of the ten months between May and April, leaving him fifty-three bushels. Let us also suppose our farmer sold five bushels of wheat in each of the ten months between the May wheat and April barley harvests. This leaves him with three bushels of wheat at the end of ten months—but wait, this is the third year and he has to make Poor Tithe in February-March, leaving him with two bushels of wheat to feed his family until the April barley harvest. However, the Passover-Unleavened Bread festival in March-April will require one of his two bushels, leaving him with one bushel to last until May. Can he do it? In modern times a bushel of wheat makes seventy-three loaves of bread (that is 584 sandwiches, which is 195 days of meals if you had a sandwich each day for breakfast, lunch, and dinner[8]). Bread and porridge (from wheat and oats) were the staple foods of the ancient world.

8. Accessed at http://montanakids.com/activitiesandgames/printandplay/Wheat_quiz.htm, on March 1, 2009

One bushel of wheat seems sufficient for one month, especially since our farmer may have other grains, fruits, and nuts in storage (bought with the money gained from selling his wheat), plus vegetables from the garden, plus any animals he may have raised or bought—and barley harvest is just around the corner. Our farmer has plenty of food to keep his family well fed until the wheat harvest is reaped, threshed, and stored in May-June, and the cycle begins anew.

Money, however, is different. Food remaining from a tithe can be eaten, supplying one of life's basic needs. Money left over after a tithe must buy everything a family needs to live in the world: food, shelter, transportation, medicine, and many other necessary things. The $22,500 remaining to each family after the ten percent tithe in our example church would leave many families struggling to live in the world. Believers understand they have a dual obligation to live in the world and support God's ministries in the world. Their giving is adjusted to meet both obligations, and is often less than required to support their local church *and* external ministries. This is why those who insist on a modern tithe must preach guilt (Malachi 3:10) to get more, and must divert much of the more they get away from the pastor in order to meet the needs of buildings, and staff, and other ministries. Again, I am not saying ministers and ministries outside the local church should not be funded. However, one must count the cost and decide if he is willing to pay it. God requires his people to give, but does not require his people to burden themselves financially in order to support others, 2 Corinthians 8:13. What is applicable to the individual church member is applicable to the membership as a church: God does not require a local church to burden themselves financially in order to support others. How much gospel ministry is a local church able and willing to support? As much as the membership is able and willing to support.

How, then, should one give to meet the needs of his pastor, his church, the poor, and other Christian ministries? Each according to his ability. Of a willing mind. More to the point, proportionate to income, according to what one has, and according to one's abundance, sharing generously and liberally, trusting God's providence, but not creating a financial burden for your family (Acts 11:29; 1 Corinthians 16:2; 2 Corinthians 8:12, 14, 15; 9:5, 6, 8, 13). How much gospel ministry is to be supported is a serious discussion churches (pastors and members) should have before they plan their yearly budget.

A Biblical Paradigm for New Testament Giving

Paul implies that the pastor's income should be equitable with his congregation's income: the tenant farmer shares in the crops he raises for the owner; the hired shepherd shares in the milk; the sower sows in the hope of sharing with the reaper; those who sow spiritual things share in material things. If, for the purposes of example only, a congregation consists of a pastor and ten families, then ten percent of each family's income will give their pastor an income that is the average of his congregation's income, which is equitable. If the congregation numbers twenty families, then five percent from each family is an equitable share. If the congregation numbers thirty families then a little over three percent of income would be required from each family to equitably support their pastor. One can see that while the individual amounts given do not matter, the total amount given must be sufficient to meet the church's obligation to its pastor. Again, a serious discussion is needed so budget reflects giving.

If the congregation has chosen, as most do, to obligate themselves to support a building, church staff, and other ministries, both within and without the local church, then more is needed—above what is needed for the pastor—to support these other needs. One church I know of has about 350 members in 140 families. Many in the church are poor, underemployed, or retired. So in this example I will again use $25,000 as an annual income. One hundred forty families earning $25,000 per year is a total annual income of $3,500,000. If each family gave one percent for the pastor, his annual income would be $35,000, which is above the congregation's average.[9] This example church has an annual budget of $406,800. Giving (in this example) must be over eleven percent of income, leaving each family with just over $22,095 to live in the world.

How much should a Christian give to support his pastor, his church's facilities and ministries, and outside ministries[10] supported by his church? New Testament giving is from the principles of a willing mind, not with sorrow or regret, but equitably, liberally, generously, and cheerfully, according to one's ability, according to what one has, not a burden, according to one's abundance. God has promised to meet his people's daily necessi-

---

9. Pastors should remember they are believers who are required to support the poor and give to other ministries.

10. If your denomination has a bishop, archbishop, etc., shouldn't their support come from the pastors—not the church members—they minister to? Wouldn't this be equitable? The churches support their pastor and the building they have chosen to worship in, shouldn't the pastors support their ecclesiastical leaders.

ties (which does not preclude testing). Therefore, believers should trust in his providence (one of the principles of giving). If God gives to meet daily necessities, which he does, then God expects his people to use what he gives to satisfy their necessary obligations; and he does. Necessary obligations are both material and spiritual: to live in the world and to support the gospel in the world.

For those wanting very specific guidance I suggest the following, based on the principles of giving proportionate to income, giving according to what one has, and giving so as to not create a financial burden for one's self and family. Make a list of all your necessary obligations, which is everything you must pay to live in the world: your home, transportation to and from your job, pharmacy, school, the food you buy, doctors, medicines, and health insurance, vehicle insurance and registration, various taxes, and all other necessary things you *must* pay.[11] Then, total the amount. Subtract this from your net income. What remains is what you have: 2 Corinthians 8:12, give according to what you have. What you can give will not burden you financially, 2 Corinthians 8:13. What remains is your abundance: 2 Corinthians 8:14, give according to your abundance. For those who want further help in determining how much they could give, see appendix four.

Those who insist on tithing money will tell you to take God's portion off the top (gross or net income) and trust God to stretch the remainder to meet your other obligations. The New Testament says that to satisfy one's debtors—rent or mortgage, utilities, food, gasoline, taxes, etc., Romans 13:7–8—is an obligation, which means having sufficient money to pay one's debts. While sacrificial giving is commended, 2 Corinthians 8:2, 3, New Testament giving does not require you to burden yourself financially in order to help others financially, 2 Corinthians 8:13, and giving is not to be with sorrow or regret over the amount, 2 Corinthians 9:5. Giving is a matter of the reaper sharing with the sower—the believer who receives spiritual things sharing his material things with the gospel minister. If one is to give willingly out of what he has (2 Corinthians 8:12), and out of his abundance (8:2, 14; 9:6, 8), then he must find out what he has so he can determine his abundance and share it liberally, generously, cheerfully: to sow bountifully so he can reap bountifully. To give bountifully,

---

11. This list is not all-inclusive. It does not, for example, include internet access for business or education (not for entertainment). Some things that may be a necessity for one may not be for another. You must decide.

2 Corinthians 9:6, does not mean a large amount of money, for this would contradict 8:12, which teaches that whatever one gives, if given willingly, it is "accepted according to what one has, not according to what he does not have." To give bountifully in this context means to give proportionately, as one purposes, as God has given sufficiency in all things, as God has given increase, as God has enriched (9:6–11). Therefore, determine what you have, figure out what you need, and give bountifully out of what God has supplied above your necessities. Remember the New Testament treats the Christian as an adult who has the spiritual maturity to figure out on his or her own how much to give. Figuring out the amount for yourself is giving according to New Testament principles.

A word of caution is necessary. What about the things one may desire? God promises, Psalm 37:4, to "give you the desires of your heart," when you "delight yourself also in the Lord." When your heart and mind seek God's will, then your desires will be in accordance with God's plans. God does not begrudge all desires—he asks for a generous share, but not all, of the abundance. However, desires that serve no purpose other than getting and having are just the sin nature lusting and being wrongfully gratified. Buying something that fills no other purpose than to satisfy one's desires spends money God gives to support his ministers and ministries. I believe this is where the New Testament believer robs God. "If we spend upon ourselves beyond bounds, if we lay out upon luxury more than is meet [appropriate], if we are superabundantly self-indulgent, and are not consecrating a fair proportion of our substance to the cause of God and the help of the poor, we are assuredly robbing the Most High."[12] Believers can act like nonbelievers, in that they can have wrongful desires. Then they may buy things they desire but do not need, or are not good for them, or that they cannot afford, and add a wrongful obligation to their necessities. To buy something one cannot afford is the worst robbery. One cannot deny that buying on credit changes a desire into an obligation to a debtor. I will address a solution to this a little later. Here, let us recognize that even a wrongful obligation is a debt that must be paid. The money that goes to pay a wrongfully incurred credit card debt, or other loan incurred for something we want but do not need, comes out of that abundance of money God gives us to meet the needs of the gospel. There is good debt and bad debt. Buying something not needed but just wanted

---

12. Charles Spurgeon, *The C. H. Spurgeon Collection*, Metropolitan Tabernacle Pulpit, vol 36, sermon 2156, July 27, 1891, "Robbers of God."

is bad debt. A mortgage or rent for a house that meets family needs is good debt; a house larger, more modern, more than needed, is a bad debt. A car that meets one's needs is a good debt; a car that satisfies one's ego is a bad debt.[13] These are big examples, but God's abundance may be given away in pennies, dimes, quarters, and dollars to satisfy wrongful desires in smaller packages. Not all desires are wrong, but care must be exercised so one does not end up robbing God to pay debt. If such a debt has been incurred, then 1) confess it as a sin and ask forgiveness; 2) stop buying desires and stick to necessities; 3) pay off the debt as quickly as possible and don't do it again; 4) trust in God to help you meet your just obligations and satisfy this wrongful debt; 5) take care to use any unexpected money for godly ends, which may include paying on, or paying off, the wrongful debt.

Finally, on this subject, one may ask, "Where is faith? If giving is not an obligation, and New Testament giving is determining the abundance 'left over' after paying one's obligations, then where does faith come in." In answer, giving is an obligation: to the pastor, to the church, to the poor. The believer is obligated to give to the gospel ministry out of his abundance. Will there be an abundance? Here is a subject for faith, for both pastor and people. Will a believer give out of his abundance? Faith again. How much of that abundance should he give? Ah, faith again! Although the believer is to give "according to what one has, not according to what he does not have," he is also to purpose in his heart to give willingly, generously, bountifully, and cheerfully. Faith is in the amount of abundance one is willing to give: is it all? is it some? One should give, says Paul, generously and bountifully, trusting—here is faith—that the providence of God will cause him to reap yet more bountifully and receive that sufficiency God gives to supply abundantly for every good work. By the way, God is not against a savings account, or investments. It was a savings account that saved Jacob and his family from the famine, Genesis 41:25–36; 42:1–2; 43:1–2; 45:5–7; 50:20. God did not object to Hezekiah's storehouse, a savings account for the agricultural tithe, he even recommended it be used, Malachi 3:10. Jesus' counsel against worry is in the sense of "be not anxious," and does not prevent the believer from planning for the future. Putting aside some

---

13. There are also addictions—alcohol, tobacco, illegal drugs, pornography, fornication—which are as much an obligation to a debt as any other wrongful desire, and therefore can also rob God.

money for savings or investment, and then deciding how that abundance may be used, that requires faith in God's blessing for the future.

PROPORTIONAL GIVING

Proportional giving is found in the New Testament principles "each lay something aside," 1 Corinthians 16:2, "give bountifully," 2 Corinthians 9:6, and "each according to his ability," Acts 11:29. The tithe also showed the principle of proportional giving. The amount one gives does have some importance in relation to the moral law of sowing and reaping. God's providence is such that, if we can trust him, he who gathers much and he who gathers a little have a sufficient amount. The principles, however, are the important things that are to guide one's giving. Giving proportional to income is both an Old and New Testament principle.[14]

A proportionate amount allows the giver to respond to the other necessary obligations of life: food, clothing, shelter, education, transportation, etc., for one's self and one's family. The believer has a dual obligation to give to God and to support the necessities of life (not specifically desires, although God is good to often give enough for lawful desires). Giving is as much an obligation as meeting other financial responsibilities—giving is a necessary financial responsibility. Proportional giving, versus a legal ten percent, allows a person to satisfy his or her obligation to give, while at the same time meeting his or her necessary financial obligations.

Proportional giving will also help the believer not get into the type of financial trouble that prevents him or her from meeting their financial obligations. That is, it can stop a person from unlawfully transforming desires into necessities. When a portion of one's income goes for life's necessities, and a portion goes to the gospel ministry, there is less a portion left to spend unwisely. Proportional giving teaches one how to wisely and biblically manage financial resources.

Proportional giving can show whether or not God is behind a particular gospel ministry or minister. If too few believers are convicted to support a ministry or its ministers, such that insufficient resources are available, then it is time for the ministry or the minister to reevaluate. On the other hand, proportional giving can be and should be sufficient

---

14. In chapter four (discussion on 1 Corinthians 16:2) proportional giving in this New Testament age was defined as a smaller percentage for a smaller income, versus a larger percentage for a larger income. The more abundance one has after meeting the expenses of living in the world, the greater percentage he should give out of that abundance.

to support those who live from the gospel, the local church, and the poor. Be a spiritually mature adult: decide what to support, give proportionally to support it.

THE IMPORTANCE OF FAITH

The Importance of Persevering Faith

The Old Testament tithe shows the importance of a persevering faith. Even though the Old Testament tithe was a set amount, various and unpredictable circumstances might cause such a low yield from the field that it might seem impossible to both tithe and sustain one's self and family. Yet, God made no provision to stop tithing when the harvest was small. The Levites, the priests, and the poor needed to eat in bad times as well as good. The tithe was to continue. Continuing to give in difficult circumstances is persevering faith.

Faith causes the things God has promised, though as yet unseen, to be a present reality to the soul. The believer does in fact by faith hold God's promises in the hand of his soul as a present reality. Persevering faith is continuing endurance that receives the promises. Men and women of faith are able to persevere under trial and disappointment because they have unshakeable confidence in the fulfillment of God's promises. Just as the Old Testament saints endured through faith (Hebrews 11) to receive the promises, even so Christians must endure through faith to receive God's promises made to them. God's promise to Old Testament believers, in relation to giving, was, Give what I have commanded and I will give what I have promised. New Testament faith for giving is not different, just expressed differently: give willingly, cheerfully, and bountifully and God will cause you to reap bountifully. Old Testament believers reaped materially and spiritually. So do New Testament believers. Some of God's promises are absolute (for example, Acts 1:11) and some are conditional. God promised Israel judgment if they forsook his Law and blessings if they obeyed the Law. God promised to pour out blessings if the people would give as commanded. Persevering faith, the subject of Hebrews 11, is possible because God keeps his promises. Faith itself is the objective presence of spiritual reality. Persevering faith begins as, and is always supported by, God-given conviction: I know God is keeping his promises because God has convicted me that he is faithful. Scripture teaches that God gives grace to persevere, grace which the believer is to receive and

A Biblical Paradigm for New Testament Giving

put to use in his or her life.[15] God gives a believer that quality of faith which results in the steadfast assurance that the promises are genuine and imminent. That kind of faith is persevering faith. There may be times and circumstances when giving is truly impossible, when lawful debts take all one's income. Persevering faith watches for an opportunity to give, and keeps sacrificial giving (see below) in mind. The Lord blesses persevering faith with receipt of the promises.

The Importance of Obedient Faith

The tithe shows the importance of an obedient faith. After he gave the rules guiding the tithes, God said nothing for 1100 years about the believer's obligation to tithe (until Malachi 3:8–10). He expected his people to be obedient and give. Malachi was God's final word on giving until the formation of the New Testament church in Acts. The Old Testament believer was obligated to tithe because the tithe was given to God through the religious system. As being given to God, giving was an act of faithful obedience. If the believer would respond with faithful obedience, God promised to bless him abundantly. The New Testament blessing for giving is part of the moral law of sowing and reaping. The blessing due Israel's obedience in Malachi 3:10 can be expressed in New Testament terms. "Give, so that those who live of the gospel may live from the gospel, so that your church may prosper, and those who are in need (the poor) may have their needs satisfied. Prove me in this, and see if I will not return abundant reaping for bountiful sowing. See if I will not open for you the windows of heaven and pour out for you such blessing that there will be more than enough for you meet your obligations and satisfy my ministers and ministries."

Sacrificial Giving

There was no sacrificial giving under the Mosaic Law. The tithe was no sacrifice. The tithe was ten percent of the agricultural product of the agrarian economy. Whether the farmer had ten thousand bushels of grain or ten bushels, the tithe was ten percent. Whether the farmer had a thousand cattle or ten cattle the tithe was ten percent. The animal, grain, and drink sacrifices offered at the altar were not giving. Those things were offered in exchange for forgiveness, or to express thanksgiving. The loss expe-

---

15. For example, Hebrews 13:5; Romans 8:28–39.

rienced in the altar sacrifices was an exchange for something of greater spiritual value. If the idea of sacrificial giving is to joyfully and freely give beyond ability, 2 Corinthians 8:3, then there was no sacrificial giving in the Mosaic economy.

Sacrificial giving is mentioned in the gift the Macedonian churches gave to Paul, 2 Corinthians 8:1–5. During a "great trial of affliction the abundance of their joy and their deep poverty abounded in the riches of their liberality." Because of the abundance of their joy, even though in great affliction and deep poverty, they were freely willing to give "according to ability, yes, and beyond ability." In so doing it was important that they first gave themselves to God and then gave their gift to Paul, 8:4–5. Paul tells the Corinthians that the Macedonian example does not mean they have to give in a manner that "others should be eased and you burdened" 8:13. Rather, Paul is using the Macedonians as an example of willingness 8:12, and cheerfulness, 9:7, in giving. When Paul was ministering in Corinth the Macedonian churches sent him several financial gifts to support his Corinthian ministry. Time had passed and now the Jerusalem church, for whom Paul had begun a collection a year ago, 8:10, was needy and the Corinthians had an abundance. It was only right that the abundantly supplied Corinthian church supply financial help to the needy Jerusalem church, just as Macedonians had earlier helped the Corinthians (by funding Paul's work in Corinth). For the Corinthians to now give out of their abundance was "an equality." Their need had been satisfied by the Macedonians; now it was their turn to help a sister church. Paul doesn't ask the Corinthians to give out of their poverty, but out of their abundance, willingly, according to what they have. Paul doesn't mean the amount the Corinthians give should equal that of the Macedonians (which was actually quite small), for he is not speaking of equity or reciprocity, but of equal relief from the burden of want. The Corinthians had been relieved by the Macedonians, and now it was time for the Corinthians to help relieve the burdens of others. God had given the Corinthians an abundance, there was a sister church in need, now was the time for the Corinthians to give out of the abundance God had given them for this very purpose, 8:15; 9:8–12.

The Macedonians had, however, freely chosen to give "beyond ability." The amount is not important: their liberality came out of deep poverty. The Greeks had two words for "poor." The *penes* poor was capable of providing for himself. The *ptochos* poor had absolutely nothing; begging

A Biblical Paradigm for New Testament Giving

was his only means of survival. The Macedonians' *ptochos* poverty was "deep," *bathos*, a word in context indicating abject poverty. They literally had nothing to give, therefore what they did give was "beyond ability." The word translated "liberality" is *haplotes*, meaning sincerity, faithfulness. In a moral sense it is the opposite of deceitful; it is being faithful toward others, helpfulness in giving assistance to others. In the 8:2 context it is "faithful benevolence out of proper motive."[16] Although in the midst of severe trials and abject poverty, the Macedonians greatly desired to participate in Paul's ministry to the Corinthians. Out of their superabundance of joy, despite their severe afflictions, they gave of themselves to God, and in the riches of their faith and deep helplessness of their poverty, they found some way to give a financial gift to Paul, a gift that was beyond the measure of their ability.[17] They had, in the words of 8:13, chosen to burden themselves in order that others might be eased. Now *that* is sacrificial giving. Putting a few extra dollars in the offering plate, or denying yourself some wanted desire in order to give extra money to Christian ministry, that is normal giving, not sacrificial giving. When one's deep and abiding joy in the midst of severe trials and deep poverty results in abundant faith toward God and faithfulness to help others, then giving is sacrificial. Put another way, the dollar amount of the gift is not relevant to the richness of the gift. "Note the paradox of poverty spilling over into wealth, which is obviously not material but relates to a richness that pertains to a generous spirit that loves to give and whose giving is not measured by the amount but by the sacrifice entailed."[18]

Sometimes believers are in circumstances where the giving they want to give is well-beyond the giving they can give. In those circumstances it is an individual choice to give sacrificially. There are also believers who have the spiritual gift of giving, which is the ability to give above and beyond normal Christian giving to further the work of the ministry of the gospel, or to help fellow believers in need. This is not sacrificial giving, but the spiritual gift of giving. As with all spiritual gifts it is empowered and guided by the Holy Spirit, who puts the person and the resources together in the right place at the right time to meet the needs of other believers and

---

16. Zodhiates, *Dictionary*, 572.

17. What they were able to give was probably slowly and painstakingly collected from begging and menial labor.

18. Martin, *2 Corinthians*, 253.

church ministries. Sacrificial giving is not a spiritual gift, but a spiritual work of faithfulness in the midst of deep affliction.

The Importance of Giving by Faith

What is faith? Faith is not believing without understanding. God wants believers to exercise a rational faith, a knowing faith, a maturing faith, and an intelligent faith. The Word of God reveals God to man, teaches sinners the way to salvation, and instructs believers how to live a holy and righteous life pleasing to God. God's Word is a testimony to rational, knowing, maturing, intelligent faith. In an illustration, faith doesn't take a step with anxiety that the next step is not there. Faith knows the way is certain, although it may not be seen, just because the Word of God says the next step is there. Faith does what God says because faith believes that what God says is true. Faith is not doing the impossible. Faith is doing what God says is possible, even when it seems impossible to us.

Faith is not giving more than I have, trusting God I will receive more than I need. Faith is giving according to what God has given me, trusting that what I have will meet every need: his and mine. Faith is managing my resources according to biblical principles. Yes, that is more complicated than "give ten percent" or "give off the top" but it is adult faith: rational, knowing, mature, intelligent faith. God didn't require the Old Testament saints to give more than they had. The faith of the Old Testament saints was, "If I give to God as he has commanded, God will give to me as he has promised." Is the New Testament different? Not according to the New Testament principles of giving. Giving by faith is "each according to his (or her) ability," Acts 11:29, "according to your abundance," 2 Corinthians 8:14, "sharing liberally," 2 Corinthians 9:13, "trusting in God's providence," 2 Corinthians 8:15; 9:8, "a matter of generosity," 2 Corinthians 9:5, "sowing bountifully to reap bountifully," 2 Corinthians 9:6, "giving proportionately," 2 Corinthians 8:12; 2 Corinthians 9:6; 1 Corinthians 16:2, "giving cheerfully, not grudgingly or of necessity," 2 Corinthians 9:7. And sometimes giving is sacrificial, when the richness of the gift is the generous spirit that loves to give and whose giving is not measured by the amount given, but in the joy and dedication that results in giving beyond ability.

In the Old Testament there were times of famine, war, diseases in plants and animals, persecution and afflictions, and giving was difficult; but the faithful believer still gave. There were times in the Old Testament

A Biblical Paradigm for New Testament Giving

when the religious system was corrupt, or ineffective, or not responsive to the spiritual needs of the people, and giving seemed a waste or undeserved; but the faithful believer still gave. Our giving is to God, not to man, but to God through man. Therefore, giving is faithful obedience to God. If we give as God has commanded, God will give as he has promised. "If anyone loves me he will keep my word; and my Father will love him," John 14:23.

Christians believe God will give as he promised because biblical faith is founded on conviction: I believe what God says is true. Conviction is the settled, unshakeable, unalterable, Holy Spirit-given assurance that God means what he says. God said it, that settles it, I will believe it and do it. Faith is inwardly believing the testimony of God (given in Scripture) through the convicting power of the Holy Spirit, and faith is outwardly acting by the power of the Holy Spirit to conform my thoughts and actions to that conviction.

Since God has not given the New Testament believer an amount he wants him to give, faith is not in the amount given, even if the amount is "sacrificial." To give is faith. To give cheerfully, abundantly, willingly, generously, liberally, and bountifully is faith, regardless of the amount given. That is because abundantly, generously, liberally, and bountifully is "according to what one has, not according to what he does not have." To give abundantly, generously, liberally, and bountifully does not mean you should be burdened and others eased. Faith is living righteously; to live righteously one must live obediently; obedience is not in the amount, but in the disposition: cheerfully and willingly; sacrificially if the occasion calls for sacrificial giving.

We receive by faith what God has given, because we believe by faith that "he who gathered much had nothing left over, and he who gathered little had no lack." We believe that "he who sows bountifully will also reap bountifully." Not specifically in the amount, but rather *not* by necessity and *not* regretfully. "Bountifully" is in the attitude—happily willing to give—as well as in the amount. Can the amount be large? Yes. Can the amount be medium-sized? Yes. Can the amount be small? Yes. Should the amount given be proportional to the amount on hand? Yes. Whatever amount one chooses to give it will leave him (or her) with less than he had. Will God make that "remainder" sufficient? The answer is yes because faith receives the promises. Can the believer trust God's love, mercy, grace, and providence? Can you adjust your desires to conform to God's will, so that what you desire is attainable, because your desire is neither more nor less than what God has willed for you? No matter how much one has, he (or she) will experience that immoral lust for more. Faith overcomes wrong desires.

Giving does not leave the believer with less than he had, it leaves him (or her) with all God has provided for all that is needed. This is faith: to live godly lives of great contentment with all God gives, trusting that what he has given is sufficient to meet our obligations, whether they be obligations to our necessary debts, to our pastor, to our church, to the poor, to our own worship needs, or to Christian ministry. Meeting every one of these needs all at one time is not faith; faith is giving to meet these needs in the priority God has given us, because that is obedience, and willing obedience is necessary to faith. Faith trusts in God to give a sufficiency to meet obligations. Faith appeals to God to teach us how to manage our money, our needs, our debts, and our giving. Faith is trusting God to supply the promised abundance, to meet the obligations he has set for us, and give us the lawful desires of our heart.

It takes faith to give material things when all one receives are intangible spiritual things. It takes faith to give willingly, cheerfully, joyfully, and equitably. It takes faith to sow bountifully, whether bountifully is two mites or beyond ability. Let no one deceive you into thinking that faith is found in the amount you give. Faith is doing what God says, not what man thinks is right.

A FINAL WORD

To Believers

Giving is a Christian obligation. If you have read this book and are saying to yourself, "Now I can keep more of my money and give less to God (my pastor, the poor, church ministries)," then you have missed the point. Giving is an obligation: those who live to preach the gospel live from the gospel; those who sow spiritual things are to reap material things from those to whom they minister. Giving is as much an obligation as paying your lawful debts. As a lawful debt owed to those who are preaching the gospel to *you*, giving should be a high priority obligation, and willingly so. As a believer concerned to fulfill Christ's command to "make disciples," giving should be an obligation willing accepted without regret. To keep more than is needed to live in the world is to rob God. God gives more

A Biblical Paradigm for New Testament Giving

so the believer can receive a blessing by supporting God's ministers, his church, and his ministries. This is how God works in the world: though you, the believer. God doesn't omnipotently zap more money into the bank accounts of ministers, churches, and ministries. He gives to others by giving through you. Some goodly portion of what you receive is meant to be given as God has commanded. If you keep more than required to live in the world, then you have disobeyed God; you have taken his blessing away from others; you have robbed God.

To Pastors and Churches

How much "church" is necessary to preach the gospel? In the early days of post-apostolic Christianity churches practiced the voluntary principle of giving. Then, as time passed, churches in the fourth century began adding more paid offices to conduct the business of the church. The writings of the church fathers indicate they sought a source with deeper pockets to pay the bishops, pastors, deacons, deaconesses, readers, singers, porters, virgins, widows, orphans, and buildings the church had obligated itself to support.[19] The church turned to the Old Testament tithe to meet the needs they had created. The tithe was not given in money, but in agricultural goods. Tithing seemed like a good plan to support new obligations. "All these [post-apostolic writings of the church fathers] demonstrate that the economic needs of the church motivated the readoption of the Old Testament laws. As the number of professional clergy increased, the more it became necessary to answer the question of how they were to be supported. Paul had established merely the basic principle that they should not have to provide for themselves. The Old Testament commandment of the tithe, then, was a welcome biblical indication as to how this was to be done."[20] The commentator misses the point: Paul did tell the church how to support its ministers. As the writings of Paul and the other apostles demonstrate, voluntary giving, not tithing, was God's plan for the church.

When the New Testament church assumed the temporal power of Imperial Rome, the church had more buildings and more people and

---

19. Is this list much different in type and intent than the bloated "ministries" one finds at a denomination headquarters? Or in large churches with multiple "pastors" being paid to do the work once done willingly by volunteers?

20. Vischer, *Tithing in the Early Church*, 29–30.

more administrative needs to support. The church turned to the lands they had inherited from the Empire, and collected land taxes and agricultural tithes from their tenant farmers. In the late eighth century Charlemagne created a unified Holy Roman Empire and added more bishops, more priests, more monks, more of everything related to the church, and enforced the tithe, AD 779. When he died (AD 814) and his empire broke apart the tithe system waned. Tithing found new life when Otto I restored the Holy Roman Empire in AD 962. From then on, the tithe system of giving reigned supreme in the Roman Catholic Church. The Reformation churches found taxes and tithes a sure way to support their new denominations. Money as a tithe began to be added, slowly but surely, and by the 1800s agricultural tithes were commuted to a money tithe. In America, the voluntary principle revived, for a time, but as churches became large denominations with more administrative positions and more educational, evangelistic, and mission-minded goals, the voluntary principle lost ground and tithed money returned. Today, although few churches and denominations directly preach a tithe, in practice they support the "principle" of ten percent.

The point is this, churches and pastors: how much "church" is needed for you to preach the gospel? Put a little differently, how many people need to be paid, how much building do you need, how many ministries outside of your local church should you support? When a local church consists of members and pastor-teachers, and all other positions are, as the New Testament teaches, voluntary and unpaid, then the members' giving to support church (people, not buildings) and pastor is sufficient to meet the needs of the local church. This is all the giving God requires of the local church. Additional giving is an obligation—voluntary to be sure—to a debt. As an example, the first missionaries, Paul and Barnabas, did not receive support from their local church. They supported themselves along the way. On later missionary endeavors Paul continued to support himself, but certain churches made a decision to send him financial support. They voluntarily took on a financial obligation to give above what God required of them to support their local church. At some time during his ministry Paul asked the churches he had help found to support a sister church. The Jerusalem church was in financial distress; it could not meet its obligations to its pastors, its members, and the poor. Paul could ask these Gentile churches to help the Jerusalem church because helping the

A Biblical Paradigm for New Testament Giving

poor is one of the three financial obligations God requires: support those who preach the gospel; provide for the church; help the poor.

Is giving to ministers and ministries other than those three local church financial obligations wrong? Of course not. If one is convicted by the Holy Spirit to give, God will provide. If one has voluntarily, willingly, cheerfully chosen to support more than his local church, then he or she should be willing and cheerful to keep less of what God gives and give more to God. That is what the voluntary principle of giving is all about: freely deciding to give, cheerfully giving. Has not God promised that he who sows bountifully will reap bountifully? Yes, and faith, having been convicted, and freely deciding to positively respond to that conviction, waits patiently to receive the promises. If we give as God has commanded or convicted, then he will give as he has promised. The Christian is a member of a super-natural religion and has a living relationship with a super-natural God. Giving is more than a financial decision, it is a faith decision; and faith responds to the instructions given in God's written Word and the conviction given by Holy Spirit, and ignores all other pleas.

Above I used an example to show how much giving was needed to support a pastor at an income approximately equal with the congregational average. I gave an example of 140 church families each earning $25,000 per year. That is a total annual income of $3,500,000. If each family gave one percent for the pastor, his annual income would be $35,000, above the congregations' average. This example church has an annual budget of $406,800. The budget includes salary for 2 pastors, a limited staff, building loan payments, many and varied internal ministries, denominational support (at several levels), missionary support, and of course building utilities and maintenance. To achieve that level of church income (using the numbers in the example), each family must give about twelve percent of their annual income. Are the 350 members in 140 families financially able—more to the point are they willing—to support this vision? This particular church hosts a local Christian school and charges them rent to make up the difference between giving and "enough church" for the vision. This is neither right nor wrong. It is simply the way this church has decided to meet the obligations imposed by its vision of gospel ministry.

Therefore, pastors and churches must ponder many questions. How much church is enough for our vision to preach the gospel? Is our vision local, national, international, global? How many people will we support to meet our vision? How will we pay for it? The example church found one solution: members giving plus renting the building. Let us take another example, common to many churches. What about a building program to attract new members and keep the old ones? Will we borrow money or save money to meet this vision? I have known churches who successfully saved money before building (or adding to) their facility. The believers in that church made a long-term commitment and carried the commitment through to completion. I have known churches who borrowed money to build (or add to) their facility and gave regularly to pay back the loan. The believers in that church made a long-term commitment and carried the commitment through to completion. Faith in God, obedience to his Word, and conviction by the Holy Spirit are the requirements for a personal and willing commitment to one's vision to see to it that the gospel is preached. These spiritual things are the things that comprise New Testament giving. How much church is enough? Only as much as you are able and willing to support to meet your vision to preach the gospel.

Appendix One

Twenty-Five Reasons New Testament Giving Is Not a Tithe

1. The tithe was a portion of the grain, fruit (including oil and wine), nuts, cattle, oxen, sheep, and goats produced by the agrarian population, Leviticus 27:30–33. Christians are never commanded to give grain, fruit, nuts, cattle, oxen, sheep, or goats.

2. Money was not tithed, Leviticus 27:30–33, but part of Christian giving is money, for example, Paul's collection for the poor in the Jerusalem church, 1 Corinthians 16:1; the Philippian church's gift to Paul (Philippians 2:25; 4:10, 15–18) to support him in Rome. Compare 2 Corinthians 8:1–5; 1 Thessalonians 4:9–10.

3. The non-agrarian population did not tithe. Every Christian is to give to support the gospel.

4. The priests did not tithe. Every Christian is a priest. Every Christian is required to support the gospel ministry.

5. The Levites and priests were paid the tithe as a wage for serving in the temple because they served in place of the other tribes, Numbers 18:1–7, 21. Every Christian is to serve the gospel and the Christian "wage" is a reward for their good works, received in heaven.

6. The Levites and priests were paid a tithe as their inheritance because they had no inheritance in the land, Numbers 18:24. The believer has an inheritance in Christ to be paid in heaven, reserved and waiting, 1 Peter 1:4.

7. The tither paid himself a tithe for use at the three mandatory festivals. There are no mandatory festivals in Christianity. Christians give to support the gospel ministry.

8. The tither tithed eight out of twelve months. The New Testament believer is give regularly.

9. The tither paid a tithe to help the poor in their local community. Christianity helps the poor locally and worldwide, for example, Galatians 2:10.

10. The tithe supported the poor once every three years. Christians are to support the poor more than every three years.

11. The tithe was used for the benefit of the congregation of Israel. Christian giving is used for ministry in the local church and worldwide.

12. The council of Acts 15 did not require Gentiles to tithe.

13. The tithe is part of the yoke of the Law Israel was unable to bear. The Jerusalem Church Council did not require Christians to bear the yoke of the Law, Acts 15:10.

14. Christians are not to be entangled with the yoke of bondage that is the Law, Galatians 5:1.

15. The Law was the divinely designed guardian to keep believers safe religiously and morally until the Christ had come. Now that faith in Christ has come, the Law is no longer needed, Galatians 5:23–25.

16. "The Law dealt with believers as children and prescribed the exact amount of giving. The gospel treats believers as men and leaves the amount to circumstances, principle, and conscience."[1]

17. No New Testament writer between Acts and Revelation (inclusive) mentions the tithe as a Christian obligation, nor as a means of supporting Christian ministry or ministers.

18. The tithe was part of a priesthood that was not perfect. The perfect priesthood of Christ does not need, receive, or take a tithe, Hebrews 7:1–11.

19. The one who receives a tithe blesses the one who gives a tithe, Hebrews 7:4–7, making the receiver positionally superior to the giver. However, all believers are equal in Christ.

---

1. Charles Bridges, *Proverbs*, 27.

Twenty-Five Reasons New Testament Giving Is Not a Tithe

20. The tithe supported a body of priests who mediated God to the people. The New Testament Church does not have a body of priests to mediate with God, because Christ is the mediator between the believer and God, and the believer is his own priest who gives himself access to God through Christ, Hebrews 10:19–22.

21. The New Testament Church does not have a body of men, the Levites, to maintain the service of the temple, because every believer is both priest and servant.

22. The elders and deacons of the New Testament Church do not function as priests and Levites. They are fellow servants with other believers, sharing equally in supporting the gospel.

23. The tithe did not support the temple, nor any of its parts. To require a tithe from the Christian to support a building is a man-made rule. Worshiping in a building is a choice. If a Christian chooses worships in a building, he or she should give to support the needs of the building.

24. When Paul had every opportunity to preach the tithe as the means of supporting the gospel, he did not, 1 Corinthians 9:9–14. Those who preach the gospel should live from the gospel, sowing spiritual things and reaping material things from those whom they serve. In this they are like the unmuzzled oxen treading out the grain who eats a little from what he provides. They are like the priests who took a portion of the sacrifices they offered on the altar.

25. The rule of giving for Christianity is to "do good and share, for with such sacrifices God is well pleased," Hebrews 13:16.

Appendix Two

Twenty-Five Reasons to Give the New Testament Way

1. Christians should give according to how they are paid in their employments. The tithe was given after every harvest was reaped.
2. Christians should adjust their giving as their economic circumstances change, for good or for ill. Harvests varied from plentiful to meager.
3. Giving should include increases such as bonuses, pay raises, dividends, etc. Abraham tithed from the spoils of war. The firstfruits of the harvest were given in addition to a tithe from the harvest.
4. Christians should use their time, money, and all their possessions to support Christian ministry. The Old Testament believer was to "Honor the Lord with your possessions," Proverbs 3:9.
5. Christians should support those who minister full time in the gospel. The tithe supported those who were devoted to minister full time to God on behalf of their fellow believers.
6. Christians should give out of their personal economic means. The tithe was the product of the economy.
7. Christians should give proportional to their income. The tithe was proportional to the production of field, tree, herds, and flocks.
8. The amount one gives is a personal choice. An exact amount was demanded by the Law, but grace frees the believer from the demands of the Law.
9. The amount Christians should give is according to their ability to give and the need required by the circumstances.
10. The amount Christians should give is according to the principle to support those who minister spiritual things and preach the gospel.

Twenty-Five Reasons to Give the New Testament Way

11. The amount Christians should give is according to conscience, that is, as the Holy Spirit convicts.

12. Christians should give purposefully, sharing themselves first, then sharing their economic means.

13. Christians should give generously, because God knows our needs and supplies them, and because God will bless one believer to meet another's needs.

14. Christians should give regularly, because ministry has regularly recurring needs.

15. Christians should give willingly, because God loves the person who gives without regret.

16. Christians should give faithfully. The amount is of less importance than abiding in the commitment to give.

17. Christians should trust in the goodness and providence of God. The Lord gives believers the necessary means to live in the world and be able to give to his ministers and ministries.

18. Christians should prioritize their giving according to their other obligations. Obligations to family come first, giving to others second.

19. Perseverance is required. There will be times when the Christian's commitment to giving will be tested, because faith is always purified and approved by trials.

20. Sacrifice may be required. A personal choice to give beyond ability is commended when giving is out of an abundance of joy in the midst of trial.

21. Christians should give locally, because the first obligation is to the congregation of the Lord.

22. God required a tithe for the poor. Christians should give to support the poor: in their congregation; in their city, in the world.

23. Christians should give globally, because the gospel command is to make disciples in all nations.

24. Christians should give wisely, because not every insistent voice is a true minister of the gospel.

Appendix Two

25. Giving is a good work. The Christian is guided in all his good works by Scripture, the Holy Spirit, and personal faith. Christian giving should be guided by Scripture, the Holy Spirit, and personal faith.

Appendix Three

Twenty-One Principles of New Testament Giving

1. Those who live for the gospel should live from the gospel, 1 Corinthians 9:14
2. Those who sow spiritual things should reap material things, 1 Corinthians 9:11
3. Those who reap support those who sow, 1 Corinthians 9:10
4. The laborer is worthy of his wages, 1 Corinthians 9:7–9; 1 Timothy 5:18
5. Out of one's income each is to lay something aside, 1 Corinthians 16:2
6. Each gives according to his own ability, Acts 11:29
7. Give proportionate to income, 1 Corinthians 16:2; 2 Corinthians 9:6
8. Give regularly, 1 Corinthians 9:13, 16:2
9. Sacrificial giving is commendable, 2 Corinthians 8:2–3
10. Giving is an offering to the Lord, 2 Corinthians 8:5
11. Giving is not by commandment, 2 Corinthians 8:8–11
12. Give from a willing mind, 2 Corinthians 8:12
13. Giving is according to what one has, 2 Corinthians 8:12
14. Do not burden yourself financially, 2 Corinthians 8:13
15. Give according to your abundance, 2 Corinthians 8:14, 15
16. Share equitably, 2 Corinthians 8:14
17. Trust in God's providence, 2 Corinthians 8:15; 9:8

Appendix Three

18. Giving is a matter of generosity, 2 Corinthians 9:5
19. Sow bountifully to reap bountifully, 2 Corinthians 9:6
20. Give cheerfully, not grudgingly or of necessity, 2 Corinthians 9:7
21. Share liberally, 2 Corinthians 9:13

Appendix Four

Christian Giving Calculator, Savings Calculator, and Income Calculator

These tables may be used as a guide to giving month by month.

The Christian Giving Calculator

Necessary Monthly Debt	JAN	FEB	MAR	APR	MAY	JUN	JUL	AUG	SEPT	OCT	NOV	DEC	Tot	Avg
Rent-Mortgage-Taxes														
Utilities (Electric/Gas/Water)														
Phone (cell phone ? necessity)														
Car Insurance														
Pharmacy														
Medical (doctor/labs/therapy)														
Dental														
Vision														
Grocery (food/household)														
Gasoline														
Education (for career)														
Internet (business/education)														
Minimum Necessary Savings														
Total Necessary Debt														
Income														
Income-Debt=Abundance														
Giving For Pastor(s)														
Giving For Church														
Giving for Poor/Other Ministries														
Abundance-Giving=for self*														

*"Remainder for Self" is God's gift to satisfy lawful desires. God does not always give more than is needed for worldly and gospel obligations. When he does allow a remainder, one should consider if it is to be used for one's self, or is there some other need (helping the poor, a special need in the church, etc.).

Minimum Necessary Savings Calculator

Save Monthly For Irregular Debt	JAN	FEB	MAR	APR	MAY	JUN	JUL	AUG	SEP	OCT	NOV	DEC	Tot	Avg (TOT/12)
Waste Pickup														
Car Registration														
Sewer														
Insurance Co-pays														
Property Taxes														
Emergency														
Maintenance (House, Car)														
Minimum Necessary Savings														

Income Calculator

Monthly Income	JAN	FEB	MAR	APR	MAY	JUN	JUL	AUG	SEP	OCT	NOV	DEC	Tot	Avg
Job 1														
Job 2														
Dividends and Interest														
Bonus														
Refunds														
Other														
Average Income														(TOT/12)

Bibliography

Aharoni, Yohanan, and Michael Avi-Yohan. *The MacMillan Bible Atlas.* rev. ed. New York, NY: Macmillan Publishing, 1968.

Alexander, Joseph Addison. *Commentary on the Acts of the Apostles.*1875. Reprinted, Grand Rapids, MI: Zondervan, 1956.

Aristotle. *Economics.* In *The Complete Works of Aristotle.* Jonathon Barnes. New Jersey: Princeton University Press, 1984.

Bangs, Nathan. *A History of the Methodist Church.* 1838. In *The Ages Digital Library, Biblical and Church History Collection.* vol. 20. CD-ROM. Rio, WI: AGES Software, Inc., 2006.

Benedict, David. *A General History of the Baptist Denomination.* 1813. In *The Ages Digital Library, Biblical and Church History Collection.* vol. 20. CD-ROM. Rio, WI: AGES Software, Inc., 2006.

Barnes, Albert. *Notes on the New Testament, 1 Corinthians.* 1884. Reprinted, Grand Rapids, MI: Baker Book House, n.d.

Berkhoff, L. *Systematic Theology.* London: Banner of Truth Trust, 1959.

Borowski, Oded. *Agriculture in Iron Age Israel.* Atlanta, GA: American School of Oriental Research, 2002.

Bridges, Charles. *A Commentary on Proverbs.* 1846. Reprinted, Edinburgh: Banner of Truth Trust, 1981.

Bromiley, G. W. gen. ed., *International Standard Bible Encyclopedia.* 4 vols. rev. ed. Grand Rapids, MI: Eerdmans Publishing, 1988.

Brown, Colin. ed. *The New International Dictionary of New Testament Theology.* Grand Rapids, MI: Zondervan, 1982.

Brown, Frances, et al. *The New Brown-Driver-Briggs-Genesius Hebrew and English Lexicon.* 1906. Reprinted, Peabody, MA: Hendrickson Publishers, 1979.

Brown, John. *An Exposition of the Epistle to the Galatians.* 1860. Reprinted, Evansville, IN: The Sovereign Grace Book Club, 1957.

Bruce, F. F. *Commentary on the Book of Acts.* The New International Commentary on the New Testament. Grand Rapids, MI: Eerdmans Publishing, 1954.

Budd, Philip J. *Numbers.* Word Biblical Commentary. Waco, TX: Word Books, 1984.

Bush, George. *Notes on Genesis.* Minneapolis, MN: James Family Christian Publishers, 1979.

Buswell, J. Oliver. *A Systematic Theology of the Christian Religion.* Grand Rapids, MI: Zondervan, 1962.

Cairns, Earle E. *Christianity Through the Centuries.* 3rd ed. Grand Rapids, MI: Zondervan, 1996.

Calvin, John. *Commentary on the Epistles of Paul the Apostle to the Corinthians.* Translated by Rev. John Pringle. 1546. Reprinted, vol 20 of *Calvin's Commentaries,* Grand Rapids, MI: Baker Book House, 1996.

Bibliography

Cansdale, George. *All the Animals of Bible Lands*. Grand Rapids, MI: Zondervan, 1970.

Cary, M., et al. *The Oxford Classical Dictionary*. 2nd ed. London: Oxford University Press, 1966.

Chafer, Lewis Sperry. *Systematic Theology*. 8 vols. 1947–1948. Reprinted, Grand Rapids, MI: Kregel Publications, 1993.

Christensen, Duane L. *Deuteronomy 1:1–21:9*. Word Biblical Commentary. Revised. Nashville, TN: Thomas Nelson Publishers, 2001.

Cripps, Richard S. *A Commentary on the Book of Amos*. 1929. Reprinted, Grand Rapids, MI: Klock & Klock Christian Publishers, 1981.

Crockett, William Day. *A Harmony of the Books of Samuel, Kings, and Chronicles*. Grand Rapids, MI: Baker Book House, 1978.

Danby, Herbert. *The Mishnah*. Oxford, England: Oxford University Press, 1933.

Durant, Will. *The History of Civilization*. Vol. 1. *Our Oriental Heritage*. New York, NY: Simon and Schuster, 1935.

Eadie, John. *Galatians*. The John Eadie Greek Text Commentaries. 1869. Reprinted, Grand Rapids, MI: Baker Book House, 1979.

Edersheim, Alfred. *The Life and Times of Jesus the Messiah*. 1883. Reprinted, Grand Rapids, MI: Eerdmans Publishing, 1971.

Edwards, Thomas Charles. *A Commentary on the First Epistle to the Corinthians*. 1885. Reprinted, Minneapolis, MN: Klock & Klock Christian Publishers, 1979.

Eliade, Mircea. *The Encyclopedia of Religion*. 16 vols. New York, NY: Macmillan Publishing, 1986.

Feinberg, Charles. *The Minor Prophets*. Chicago, IL: Moody Press, 1978.

Gesenius' Hebrew and Chaldee Lexicon. Translated by Samuel Tragelles. 1847. Reprinted, Grand Rapids, MI: Baker Book House, 1979.

Getz, Gene A. *A Biblical Theology of Material Possessions*. Chicago, IL: Moody Press, 1990.

Godet, Frederic Lewis. *Commentary on First Corinthians*. 1889. Reprinted, Grand Rapids, MI: Kregel Publications, 1977.

Grudem, Wayne. *Systematic Theology*. Grand Rapids, MI: Zondervan, 1994.

Grun, Bernard. *The Timetables of History*. New York, NY: Simon and Schuster, 1979.

Guthrie, Donald. *Hebrews*. Tyndale New Testament Commentaries. Grand Rapids, MI: Eerdmans Publishing, 1983.

Harris, Laird R., et al. *Theological Wordbook of the Old Testament*. 2 vols. Chicago IL: Moody Press, 1980.

Hasting, James. *Encyclopedia of Religion and Ethics*. 13 vols. New York, NY: Charles Scribner's Sons, 1908–1922 (Index, 1927).

Henry, Matthew. *Matthew Henry's Commentary on the Whole Bible*. vol 6. Old Tappen, NJ: Fleming H. Revell Company, n.d.

Henry, Matthew, and Thomas Scott. *Commentary on the Holy Bible*. 3 vols. Nashville, TN: Thomas Nelson Publishers, 1979.

Hodge, Charles. *An Exposition of the First Epistle to the Corinthians*. 1857. Reprinted, Grand Rapids, MI: Eerdmans Publishing, 1980.

———. *An Exposition of the Second Epistle to the Corinthians*. 1859. Reprinted, Grand Rapids, MI: Baker Book House, 1980.

———. *Systematic Theology*. 3 vols. 1871–73. Reprinted, Grand Rapids, MI: Eerdmans Publishing, 1981.

Hollingsworth, David R. *Biblical Chronology*. Self published, 2008.

Bibliography

Josephus. *The Works of Flavius Josephus.* Translated by William Whiston. Philadelphia, PA: Porter and Coates, n.d.

Keener, Craig S. *Revelation.* NIV Application Commentary. Grand Rapids, MI: Zondervan, 2000.

Keil, C. F., and F. Delitzsch. *Commentary on the Old Testament.* 1866–91. Vol. 1. Reprinted, Peabody, MA: Hendrickson Publishers, 1996.

Kelly, J. N. D. *Early Christian Doctrines.* Peabody, MA: Prince Press, 2003.

Kelly, William. *Notes on the First Epistle to the Corinthians.* Denver, CO: Wilson Foundation, n.d.

Kittle, Gerhard, and Gerhard Friedrich. *Theological Dictionary of the New Testament.* 10 vols. Translated by Geoffrey W. Bromiley. Grand Rapids, MI: Eerdmans Publishing, 1967.

Kurtz, J. H. *Sacrificial Worship of the Old Testament.* 1863. Reprinted, Minneapolis, MN: Klock & Klock Christian Publishers, 1980.

Ladd, George Eldon. *A Theology of the New Testament.* rev. ed. Grand Rapids, MI: Eerdmans Publishing, 1993.

Latourette, Kenneth Scott. *A History of Christianity.* 2 vols. rev. ed. San Francisco, CA: HarperSanFrancisco, 1975.

———. *Christianity in a Revolutionary Age, A History of Christianity in the Nineteenth and Twentieth Centuries.* 5 vols. Grand Rapids, MI: Zondervan, 1969.

Lenski, R. C. H. *The Interpretation of St. Paul's First and Second Epistle to the Corinthians.* 1937. Reprinted, Columbus, OH: Wartburg Press, 1946.

Leonard, Bill J. *Early American Christianity.* Nashville, TN: Broadman Press, 1983.

Lightfoot, J. B. *The Apostolic Fathers, Clement, Ignatius, and Polycarp.* Edited and translated by J. B. Lightfoot. 1889. Vol. 2. Reprinted, Peabody, MA: Hendrickson Publishers, 1989.

Longenecker, Richard N. *Galatians.* Word Biblical Commentary. Waco, TX: Word Books, 1990.

Luther, Martin. *The Complete Sermons of Martin Luther.* 7 vols. Grand Rapids, MI: Baker Book House, 2000.

Marshall, I. Howard. *New Testament Theology.* Downers Grove, IL: InterVarsity Press, 2004.

Martin, Ralph P. *2 Corinthians.* Word Biblical Commentary. Waco, TX: Word Books, 1986.

Maspero, G. *The Dawn of Civilization: Egypt and Chaldea.* 1894. Online: http://www.archive.org.

McClintock, John, and James Strong. *Cyclopedia of Biblical, Theological, and Ecclesiastical Literature.* 1895. In *The Ages Digital Library, Cyclopedia of Biblical, Theological, and Ecclesiastical Literature.* CD-ROM. Rio, WI: AGES Software, Inc., 2000.

Melton, J. Gordon. *American Religious Creeds.* 3 vols. New York, NY: Triumph Books, 1991.

Morgan, G. Campbell. *The Westminster Pulpit.* 1906–1916. Vol. 4. Reprinted, Grand Rapids, MI: Baker Book House, n.d.

———. *The Corinthian Letters of Paul.* New York, NY: Fleming H. Revell Company, 1946.

Morris, Leon. *1 Corinthians.* Tyndale New Testament Commentaries. 1958. Reprinted, Grand Rapids, MI: Eerdmans Publishing, 1999.

Bibliography

Mounce, William D. *Pastoral Epistles*. Word Biblical Commentary. Nashville, TN: Thomas Nelson Publishers, 2000.

Philo. *Works*. Translator C. D. Yonge, Peabody, MA: Hendrickson Publishers, 1993.

Poole, Matthew. *A Commentary on the Holy Bible*. Vol. 3. McLean VA: MacDonald Publishing Company, n.d.

Powell, Milton B. *The Voluntary Church, American Religious Life, 1740–1860, Seen Through the Eyes of European Visitors*. New York, NY: The Macmillan Company, 1967.

Ramsay, William M. *Historical Commentary on First Corinthians*. Edited by Mark Williams. Grand Rapids, MI: Kregel Publications, 1996.

Roberts, Alexander, and James Donaldson. *Ante-Nicene Fathers*. Vol. 1. *The Apostolic Fathers, Justin Martyr, Irenaeus*. 1885. Reprinted, Peabody, MA: Hendrickson Publishers, 1995.

———. *Ante-Nicene Fathers*. Vol. 2. *Fathers of the Second Century: Hermas, Tatian, Athenagoras, Theophilus, and Clement of Alexandria (Entire)*. 1885. Reprinted, Peabody, MA: Hendrickson Publishers, 1995.

———. *Ante-Nicene Fathers*. Vol. 7. *Lanctantius, Venantius, Asterius, Victorinus, Dionysius, Apostolic Teaching and Constitutions, 2 Clement, Early Liturgies*. 1886. Reprinted, Peabody, MA: Hendrickson Publishers, 1995.

Robertson, Archibald, and Alfred Plummer. *A Critical and Exegetical Commentary on the First Epistle to the Corinthians*. International Critical Commentary. 1914. Reprinted, Edinburgh: T. & T. Clark 1967.

Ryrie, Charles C. *Biblical Theology of the New Testament*. Chicago, IL: Moody Press, 1959.

Schaff, Philip. *Nicene and Post-Nicene Fathers, First Series*. Vol. 6. *Augustin: Sermon on the Mount, Harmony of the Gospels, Homilies on the Gospels*. 1888. Reprinted, Peabody, MA: Hendrickson Publishers, 1999.

———. *Nicene and Post-Nicene Fathers, First Series*. Vol. 13. *Chrysostom: Homilies on Galatians, Ephesians, Philippians, Colossians, Thessalonians, Timothy, Titus, Philemon*, 1889. Reprinted, Peabody, MA: Hendrickson Publishers, 1999.

———. *History of the Christian Church*. 8 vols. 1910. Reprinted, Grand Rapids, MI: Eerdmans Publishing, 1955.

———. *The Creeds of Christendom*. 3 vols. 1931. Reprinted, Grand Rapids, MI: Baker Book House, 1983.

Schaff, Philip, and Henry Wace, *Nicene and Post-Nicene Fathers, Second Series*. Vol. 11. *Sulpitius Severus, Vincent of Lerns, John Cassian*. 1894. Reprinted, Peabody, MA: Hendrickson Publishers, 1999.

———. *Nicene and Post-Nicene Fathers, Second Series*. Vol. 12. *Leo the Great, Gregory the Great*. 1895. Reprinted, Peabody, MA: Hendrickson Publishers, 1999.

Schurer, Emil. *The History of the Jewish People in the Age of Jesus Christ*. 6 vols. rev. ed. Edinburgh: T. & T. Clark, 1979.

Scroggie, William G. *The Unfolding Drama of Redemption*. Grand Rapids, MI: Zondervan, 1976.

Shedd, W. G. T. *Dogmatic Theology*. 1863. 3 vols. Reprinted, Nashville, TN: Thomas Nelson Publishers, 1980.

———. *History of Christian Doctrine*. 2 vols. 1889. Reprinted, Minneapolis, MN: Klock & Klock Christian Publishers, 1978.

Smith, Billy K., and Frank S. Page. *Amos, Obadiah, Jonah*. The New American Commentary. Nashville, TN: Broadman & Holman Publishers, 1995.

Bibliography

Spurgeon, Charles H. *The Ages Digital Library, C. H. Spurgeon Collection.* Version 2.0. CD-ROM. Rio WI: Ages Software, Inc., 2001.

Stuart, Douglas. *Hosea-Jonah.* Word Biblical Commentary. Nashville, TN: Thomas Nelson Publishers, 1987.

The Apocrypha, An American Translation. Translated by Edgar J. Goodspeed. 1938. Reprinted, NY: Vintage Books, 1989.

Thomas, W. H. Griffith. *The Principles of Theology.* 4th ed. London: Church Room Book Press Ltd., 1951.

Towner, Philip H. *The Letters to Timothy and Titus.* New International Commentary on the New Testament. Grand Rapids, MI: 2006

Unger, Merrill F. *Unger's Bible Dictionary.* Chicago, IL: Moody Press, 1975.

Vine, W. E. *1 Corinthians.* 1951. Reprinted, Grand Rapids, MI: Zondervan, 1965.

Vischer, Lukas. *Tithing in the Early Church.* Translated by Robert C. Schultz. Philadelphia, PA: Fortress Press, 1966.

Watson, Thomas. *A Body of Divinity.* 1692. Reprinted, Grand Rapids, MI: Baker Book House, 1979.

Wenham, Gordon J. *Genesis 1-15.* Word Biblical Commentary. Waco, TX: Word, 1987.

Wilson, William. *Wilson's Old Testament Word Studies.* Virginia: MacDonald Publishing, n.d.

Zodhiates, Spiros. ed. *The Complete Word Study Dictionary New Testament.* Revised. Chattanooga, TN: AMG Publishers, 1993.

www.ingramcontent.com/pod-product-compliance
Lightning Source LLC
Chambersburg PA
CBHW051936160426
43198CB00013B/2179